PRAISE FOR *EFFECTIVE IMMEDIATELY*

"This book is filled with invaluable wisdom from authors who have led and inspired others. It's that increasingly rare book—written with respect for our time with brevity, clarity, energy, and wit. What more could a reader ask for?"

—HARRY BECKWITH, bestselling author of *Selling the Invisible* and *You, Inc.*

"The perfect resource to help college graduates launch a successful career."

—BRAD SMITH, president and chief executive officer, Intuit

"*Effective Immediately* shows recent college graduates how to be key players at work by providing them with the necessary tools to successfully manage their professional image, their relationships with coworkers and their boss, and ultimately their career trajectory."

—SHAWN GRAHAM, director of MBA Career Services, University of Pittsburgh, and author of *Courting Your Career*

"An essential resource for young professionals that bridges the gap between what you can't learn in college—and what you need to know to succeed on the job."

—GASTON CAPERTON, president, the College Board (creator of the SAT® and Advanced Placement Program®)

"This book packs a wallop of practical wisdom for young rookies determined to make it to the all-stars."

—ROBYN WATERS, author of *The Trendmaster's Guide* and *The Hummer and the Mini*

"A no-nonsense guide to finding your place in the world and maintaining a powerful presence at work that yields extraordinary results and keeps you ahead of the pack."

—DAN SCHAWBEL, personal branding expert and author of *Me 2.0*

"*Effective Immediately* tells it the way it is. Written in a way that young professionals will recognize and respect, this book offers dozens of practical lessons on getting ahead—agenda-free—in your first job out of college. Grads will learn a lot and have a few good laughs in the process."

—ALEXANDRA LEVIT, author of *They Don't Teach Corporate in College* and *New Job, New You*

EFFECTIVE IMMEDIATELY

EFFECTIVE IMMEDIATELY

How to FIT IN, STAND OUT, and MOVE UP at Your First REAL JOB

EMILY BENNINGTON and SKIP LINEBERG

TEN SPEED PRESS
Berkeley

Dedicated to young professionals who will be the change they want to see in the workplace.

Copyright © 2010 by Emily Bennington and Skip Lineberg

All rights reserved.
Published in the United States by Ten Speed Press, an imprint of the Crown Publishing Group, a division of Random House, Inc., New York.
www.crownpublishing.com
www.tenspeed.com

Ten Speed Press and the Ten Speed Press colophon are registered trademarks of Random House, Inc.

Library of Congress Cataloging-in-Publication Data
Bennington, Emily.
  Effective immediately : how to fit in, stand out, and move up at your first real job / Emily Bennington and Skip Lineberg. — 1st ed.
      p. cm.
  Includes bibliographical references and index.
  Summary: "A guide for recent college graduates and other new professionals on how to excel at their first job and jump-start their career. Includes advice about earning the respect of superiors and colleagues, staying organized, coping with mistakes, and more, plus words of wisdom from former 'newbies'"—Provided by publisher.
  1. Career development. 2. Vocational guidance. 3. Success in business.
4. College graduates—Employment. I. Lineberg, Skip. II. Title.
  HF5381.B3625 2010
  650.1—dc22

                              2010002941

ISBN 978-1-58008-999-9

Printed in the United States of America

Design by Betsy Stromberg
Cover photograph copyright © by iStockphoto.com / -Antonio-
Photograph on page 34 copyright © by iStockphoto.com / scol22

10 9 8 7 6 5 4 3

First Edition

CONTENTS

PART TWO

Score Major-League Points When You're Still a Rookie . . . 47

PART THREE
Earn Unbridled Respect from Your Boss, Colleagues, and Clients . . . 77

PART SIX
Become a Skilled, Nontoxic Leader . . . 185

ACKNOWLEDGMENTS

From Emily

A very special thank-you to the following individuals who have been with me from the start of this journey:

Johnny Tugwell, for the unconditional support of my wacky ideas—and the freedom to pursue them.

Skip Lineberg, for being the inspiration behind this project. Every newbie should be lucky enough to have a friend and mentor like you.

Rick Frishman, for all of the invaluable advice that set us on the right path.

Michael Hetzer, for being a remarkable teacher and early sounding board.

My family, who thought the prospect of actually getting published so implausible they called this "the project" for years.

My grandmother, Mary Lou Bennington, for always reminding me what is most important in life.

Christian and Liam, future graduates, who will always be standouts in my eyes.

From Skip

This book would not have been possible without the help and support of many people, including my wife, Lisa Sherman Lineberg, a great leader from whom I have learned so much. Thanks to my wonderful, loving children, Chloe and Sherman; it is for you and for your bright future that I burned so many barrels of midnight oil and came home after family supper so many evenings. Thanks to my parents, Deanna and Paul Culler, for their unwavering love and support and for raising me well, teaching me, providing for me, and shaping my values.

Thanks to my business partners, Steve Haid, Michael Haid, and Jim Nester, for many valuable lessons and for allowing me the freedom and flexibility to complete this project while helping to run Maple Creative. Thanks to my coauthor, Emily Bennington, my protégée who is also my teacher, partner, and friend. Thanks to Carrie Bowe for providing much-needed early proofing, editing, and advice.

I also want to recognize several of my teachers from the public schools of Berkeley County, West Virginia, each of whom left an impression on me and taught me so much: Dorothy Clohan, Sam Lucas, Dale Hicks, Bryan Swisher, Ken Detterer, June West, Butch Yurish, and Bob Kamensky. Special credit and thanks go to my college advisor and mentor, Dr. Jack Byrd of the College of Engineering at West Virginia University; his white paper "Understanding Young Professionals" provided a tremendously valuable seed of enlightenment that inspired a magazine article and much of the content for this book.

Thanks to my dear friend and client, Dr. David Clayman, a gifted psychologist and communicator who helps many of us make sense of an often crazy world; he is the soul and voice of our West Virginia community.

I also want to thank and recognize the bosses for whom I've worked and from whom I have learned so much: Jack Crew, Rick Linder, Jim Ambrose, John Barth, and Greg Skeen at GE; Andy Flores, Ben Garland, John Snider, and Tom Burns (God rest his soul) at the West Virginia Development Office; and Bill Goode at BIDCO, perhaps the greatest boss of them all. Finally, I want to recognize my mentors: Gaston Caperton, former governor of West Virginia; Newton Thomas, who instilled in me the passion for community service; and John Wells (God rest his soul), who taught me about being a man and a leader of men.

From Both

Finally, thanks to:

Our agent, Linda Konner, for taking a chance—and for bird-dogging "the project" until it found a good home.

Our copyeditor, Kristi Hein, and proofreader, Kim Catanzarite—thank you for your creativity, your uncanny knowledge of proper grammar, and for challenging us to write with the best reader in mind.

All our friends at Ten Speed Press, particularly our designer, Betsy Stromberg.

And Genoveva Llosa, Lisa Westmoreland, and especially Ashley Thompson. We thought it would be tough to find one editor who truly understood our vision—but we found three!

INTRODUCTION

To move up, you must get noticed.
To get noticed, you must attract attention.
To attract attention, you must be distinctive.
To be distinctive, you must be known for results.

As a new professional, learning *how* to be a professional is your first task. Whatever career or industry you choose, if you want to be respected by colleagues, invaluable to clients, and a crackerjack to your boss, mastery of the basics of business is essential.

Effective Immediately is designed to teach you how to survive your first year in the workforce. But we want to do more than that—we want you to become *great*. In a world overrun by the so-so and the okay, excellence wins, but it's a choice you have to make every day. Long-term success—the only kind that really matters—never just happens; it is always the result of clear objectives, laser focus, and building good work habits from day one.

So if you want to be an extraordinary executive, this is your book. If you're an enthusiastic, curious sort who is unimpressed by generic catchphrases and who wants—make that *demands*—to know how to be the best, this is your book.

The principles on these pages, if applied correctly, will elevate you to the top of your game. In fact, by the time you need to order new business cards, you should already have been promoted. And that's not hyperbole, just great business.

To your success,

Emily Bennington   Skip Lineberg

A CONTRACT BETWEEN YOU AND ÜBER-YOU

I, _____, understand that this is a critical time in my career when first impressions matter. I promise to stack the odds in my favor as much as possible by arriving at work on time every day, meeting all assigned deadlines, taking ownership of my projects, and continually asking myself, "If it were *my* business, would this be acceptable?"

Pursuant to same, I pledge to use this time to earn the trust and respect of my peers and subordinates. I recognize that when I am promoted to a management position, I will be responsible for leading these very colleagues.

I acknowledge that this contract is between me and myself and carries no rewards or penalties apart from accelerated success, faster promotions, and my own personal transformation from new graduate to first-class executive.

_____   _____

Signature   Date

PART ONE

Get It Right, Right Out of the Gate

FROM YOUR VERY FIRST DAY on the job, you are being evaluated by supervisors and colleagues. Will they judge you as a rank-and-file associate or a potential leader?

The answer is often determined by the first impressions you make. And it doesn't matter whether you are the world's most productive, intelligent new professional—if you are perceived differently, your career will suffer.

1 / Conquer Your First Day

Here we are, folks: the first day. And right now, you are under the microscope. Since your supervisors can't judge you on performance and contributions yet, the focus will be on filling out piles of paperwork, getting you situated, and integrating you into the team. But make no mistake, *you are being judged*.

However, instead of the usual measures that will kick in once you're settled into the position, you will be judged on some very visible, basic parameters:

- Did you show up on time?
- What are you wearing?
- Do you display confidence and charisma?
- Do you seem overwhelmed or ready for a challenge?
- How well do you communicate?
- What personal items did you put in your office?

On the first day, your mission is simple: Make a positive first impression. And the way to do that is to be very *intentional* about how you present yourself. Here are some tips that will help you not merely survive your first day, but conquer it with poise and professionalism.

Arrive Early

Make sure you are on-site at least ten to fifteen minutes before your official start time. If your commute involves driving or taking public transportation, consider rehearsing your route in advance. (Try to go when travel conditions are as realistic as possible; for instance, don't make the drive on a Sunday afternoon if you'll be traveling during weekday morning rush hour.) Giving yourself a bit of extra time will not only create some leeway if there are any unexpected delays (traffic, parking, and so on), but will also let you step into the restroom and collect yourself once you arrive. You'll be understandably nervous, so don't let normal first-day jitters spiral into outright panic by getting behind schedule.

Look the Part

The saying "Dress for the job you want, not the one you have" applies from your very first day at work. While every office is different and some are more casual than others, a good rule of thumb is to dress a notch above your current station. For most new employees, this means donning a high-quality, conservative suit that's pressed and spotless, wearing shoes that are polished, and carrying a leather (or faux leather) briefcase or messenger bag. To save time on your big day, have your outfit ready the night before. Also, don't forget to bring a pack of breath mints. Even the sharpest suit can be forgotten next to someone who smells like day-old Starbucks.

Exude Confidence

This is truly a crossroads in your life and the first step to building an extraordinary career. You're earning your own money now, and there's no limit to what you can achieve. Regardless of your past work or life experiences, this is an opportunity to start fresh and turn the page. Embrace it and walk tall.

Take Initiative

A great way to come across as friendly and confident right away is to proactively introduce yourself to your new colleagues. Don't assume they should reach out to you first because it's their workplace already. Just extend a firm handshake, smile warmly, and have some fifteen-second "about me" sound bites ready. Take some time beforehand to think about the questions you are likely to be asked and be prepared with insightful, succinct responses. In fact, we'll make it easy—you're probably going to be asked about:

- Your university (and its latest football record)
- Your major
- Your professors (if you encounter any alumni)
- Your hometown
- Your current role ("So, you're our new associate, eh?")
- Your tasks (If you don't yet know what types of projects you'll be assigned, just smile and say, "I'm not sure exactly what I'll be working on yet, but I'm looking forward to getting started.")

Also, since you're going to be doing lots of introductions, come up with some questions for your coworkers so the conversation is a dialogue rather than a Q & A session. You can research key players online via the company website, Google, or LinkedIn, but if all else fails, look around their office for clues on topics of interest. For example, if the walls are dripping with plaques, comment on one. If their desk is filled with family photos, ask about their children.

The point here is to realize that the impressions you're making on the job don't have to be left to chance. In PR, they call this "controlling the message." You can call it being *effective immediately*. Are you ready? Welcome to the workforce!

Leave the Sequins and Pleather at Home

My first real job was for a company owned by the world's largest fashion conglomerate and located in America's fashion capital, New York City. I figured I had "made it" and needed to look the part. I researched all of the major fashion magazines for the latest trends and developed a work wardrobe of gold pleather pants, brightly colored tops, and excessive chunky jewelry. I even took a day-to-night approach by wearing a sequined tank that would look great after work and toning it down for the office by pairing it with simple black pants. It only took a short time to notice that no one else in the office was wearing sequins or gold pants, and that I had mistaken trendy looks from the magazines' pages for chic business attire. I realized then that if I wanted to be treated like a professional, I had to dress accordingly.

Nicole Lemoine
Public educator
New York, New York

2 / Have Patience

Fresh out of college, many newbies think that because of their education they have immediate status and deserve lofty positions. Not so. Status is the result of accomplishment, which is the result of work. Hard, often tedious work.

Any time you are a new hire, and especially at the beginning of your career, you must build your own success from the ground up. Do not expect anyone to assume you're talented. You have to *show* them—and this takes time. Usually more time than you expect.

So be patient. Don't focus on *when* you're going to move up; focus on *what* you're doing now. As Sir William Osler (a pioneer of modern medicine) stated, "The best preparation for tomorrow is to do today's work superbly well." If at the end of each workday you can truthfully say that you worked to the best of your ability, we guarantee your success will take care of itself.

3 / Mind Your "-Ilities"

To: Entry-Level Associates
From: The Boss
Re: Mind Your "-Ilities"

Management would like to take this opportunity to welcome all of you aboard. We are thrilled that you have chosen to work for our organization, and we know that you will be a great asset to the team.

Having said that, we would also like you to be aware that all respective department heads are now actively scouting for the company's next "young guns." And while other newbies will have orientation as usual (that is, they'll be given the tour and then left alone), young guns will be handpicked for the fast track. They will be carefully groomed for big chairs in the executive suite and will be first in line for promotions, top projects, personal attention, and other perks.

If you want to become a member of the club, management recommends that you stack the odds in your favor by minding your "-ilities" (dependability, reliability, humility, accountability, responsibility, likeability, punctuality, and so on). Until we've had enough time to sufficiently evaluate the caliber of your work, our first impressions of you will be based on perceptible qualities, like "-ilities," we can see for ourselves. Just thought you should know.

Sincerely,
The Boss

4 / Prepare for the Brain Dump

Fact: When you're new, you're going to be overwhelmed. Everyone who seemingly knows *everything* about your office and its customers is going to randomly "dump" this knowledge on you in rapid, shotgun-like outbursts. Usually these brain dumps occur in stream-of-consciousness statements that begin on your first day, often before you've had a chance to locate the coffee maker. ("Ann will be your main client contact, but she's out of the office on Tuesdays and every other Thursday. Here's the supply closet; if you can't find something here, there's another located on the fifth floor. There are separate recycling containers for paper, cardboard, glass, and plastic— and all paper recyclables must be totally staple-free. What were we talking about a minute ago?")

It's a lot to take in at once, but rest assured, the brain dump happens to everyone. Prepare yourself by knowing that you *will* be bombarded with new people and new information coming at you from every direction. However, there are a few things you can do to manage the flow.

Study Your Business

In your first few days on the job, carve out some time to research everything you can about your company and how it operates. Explore your website, read your organization's marketing brochures, annual reports, and proposals. Without breaching security policies, search around the intranet and read any reports, timelines, work plans, and other relevant documents you can find. Copy the best of these to your desktop, then format your work to look similar. This background will most likely answer a lot of the more basic questions that every new employee asks, so you can stand out with more targeted, insightful observations.

But Do Ask Questions—Even Basic Ones

When you're new, you have about a two-week grace period in which coworkers will cheerfully answer any inane question you throw at them. Take advantage of this time now and use it to your benefit. Later on, they may not be so charitable.

Get Organized

When it comes to taking notes, it's critical to keep everything in one place. Therefore you'll want to carry your planner or a notebook with you at all times—you never know when the next brain dump will take place. (See pages 22–23 for some note-taking tips.) Also, if you work at a job where you're responsible for multiple projects at the same time, start a new page for each one. This will give you space to go back and add notes as needed.

Stay Sane

Never allow the brain dump to visibly stress you out. Remember, people are still forming impressions of you at this point; if you can't handle the first week without being completely overwhelmed, they're naturally going to wonder whether you're cut out for the job. In truth, brain dumps usually occur because most of your colleagues haven't thought much about your arrival before you showed up, so they're just spouting information as it comes to them. At the end of the day, take as many notes as you can, smile often, and know that in a few months you will be brain dumping on the next wide-eyed newbie—just remember to let them have some coffee first.

5 / Don't Expect a Lot of Hand-Holding

Regardless of where you work or what industry you're in, there are certain processes, tools, and forms that make up the standard operating procedures of your company. Perhaps you were introduced to these through a very organized, systematic orientation. If so, great—consider yourself fortunate. If not, don't feel shortchanged or frustrated. Instead, take initiative and master the basics on your own.

In decades past, when most people worked for huge corporations, the training process for newcomers was given greater attention. Fully staffed human resource departments handled orientation, or mid-level managers or supervisors were responsible for getting new hires up to speed.

Today, things are different. Companies have pared back layers of management and administrative functions to become leaner and more competitive. Traditional HR departments are either gone or spread thin. In addition, the world is becoming increasingly populated by small businesses, many of which have not yet developed structured processes for training new employees. As a result, basic procedures like orientation get less direct attention. (And this trend is not likely to reverse.)

So don't wait for orientation to come to you. Go out and tackle it yourself. Ask your colleagues for help. (Be patient and persistent, though; providing this information may not be anyone's direct responsibility.) The following chapter includes lists of questions that are typically addressed during more formal orientations.

6 / What You Need to Know in the First Few Weeks

Some companies will provide new employees with an orientation manual that deals with many of the topics below, both macro and micro. It is unlikely, however, that the manual will cover *all* of them. Since the answers to these questions are essential, we recommend that you transfer the relevant content to a notebook, binder, or Word document. As you learn more about a certain topic, add the information to your files along with any pertinent forms or reports.

Regardless of your method, make sure that you're well-informed about all of the key issues that affect you as an employee. If a few weeks pass and you still have unanswered questions or are unclear about something, talk to your supervisor or the HR department. (It may seem awkward at first, but your boss will most likely be impressed by your attention to detail and initiative to address any unresolved matters.)

Macro Picture Checklist

1. What are the key responsibilities of your job?
2. How will your individual performance be evaluated? How often and by whom?
3. What are the performance measurements by which your team or division is judged?
4. What are your sales, revenue, service, or productivity goals?
5. Who are your company's key customers or clients?
6. What are your company's target industry sectors or focus areas?

7. Who are your company's primary competitors?

8. What is your expected career path, including typical progression, advancement, alternatives, and expected time frames?

Micro Picture Checklist

1. Who is the supervisor or boss you report to directly, and who does that person report to?

2. Where do you obtain business cards, company stationery, and supplies?

3. How do you purchase supplies or services, and who must approve these transactions?

4. Are there any reports or forms that your supervisor requires you to submit? What are the desired formats and due dates?

5. If you need to submit an accounting of your hours worked, what's the policy?

6. When will you become eligible for benefits such as insurance, paid vacation, savings programs, and health-care coverage? How do you sign up for them?

7. How do you request leave or time off?

8. Will you be required to travel? How do you submit your travel expenses?

9. How do you handle a complaint or claim from a customer?

10. What are your company's fiscal year and business reporting cycles?

Figuring out the answers to these questions may seem like a considerable undertaking—and indeed it is. But given the issues at stake, what could be more important? Here is your first opportunity to be a top performer. Go shine.

7 / A Crash Course in Professional Etiquette

If you want to successfully operate on the same level as your company's top executives, you must observe the rules. The following are general courtesies that should serve you well in most business situations.

Universal

- Never be caught without a business card. If you don't want to carry around an official case, keep a few cards in your wallet.
- Never interrupt your boss or colleagues when they are speaking. (This includes finishing sentences.)
- Stand when a senior executive enters the room. Sometimes this will involve a bit of corporate theater; for instance, you *begin* to stand, giving the other person an opening to wave you down.
- Listen more than you talk—and resist the temptation to fill awkward conversation gaps with awkward conversation. The uncomfortable silence is always better than saying something silly you may regret later.
- Even if a coworker is wearing the most heinous article of clothing you've ever seen, resist the temptation to comment on it—or laugh along with others who do.
- Always clean up after yourself in the kitchen, make a new pot of coffee when you take the last cup, report a machine that isn't working properly (instead of abandoning it for someone else to deal with), and so on.
- If you wouldn't use certain words with your grandmother, don't use them in a work setting.

- If a senior executive calls a meeting with you, arrive early. It's rude to keep someone who outranks you waiting.

- If a colleague has something stuck in his teeth or an unzipped fly, pull him aside and politely point it out. (Imagine how embarrassed you would feel if *you* had been talking to a client and found out later that you had a giant broccoli floret sprouting out of your mouth.)

- Never criticize a coworker in public or in front of other colleagues.

- Unless you're physically impaired or want to be seen as remarkably lazy, don't take the elevator to go up or down one floor.

- Don't create excess noise or distractions in the workplace. Keep your voice down when talking on the phone and don't force coworkers to listen to your music. Even if they are too polite to say anything to you directly, you're probably getting on their nerves.

- If anyone farts (including you), ignore it.

At a Business After-Hours or Social Event

- Always wear your nametag on the *right*. This makes it easier for others to read when you're shaking hands. Not to mention, every smug executive who knows this rule notices others who don't.

- Never have more than one drink. (It's also a good idea to avoid ordering cocktails with names that sound like X-rated film titles.)

- Avoid *over*-hugging and indiscriminate cheek kissing. If you know someone well, a hug or a peck on the cheek is acceptable. If not, politely shake hands and leave it at that.

- If the food looks messy, leave it alone.

At a Business Dinner

- Before the dinner, try to read your local newspaper, a recent trade journal, and the latest issue of *Newsweek* or *Time* magazine. Also, if you're entertaining a prospect or client, be sure to Google them in advance. You never know where the conversation will go, and it's best to have a few topics at the ready.

- It's okay to try and sit close to the bigwigs, but don't jockey for a seat right beside them unless you're asked. This is a privilege typically reserved for clients, higher-ranking colleagues, or visiting guests.

- Remember: bread on the left, water on the right. A common trick to recall this is the acronym BMW, which gives you a left-to-right table layout of bread, meal, water. Also, bread is always passed counterclockwise.

- If you don't understand anything about wine, don't pretend that you do. The follow-up questions from dinner guests will out you every time.

- When it comes to ordering, take your cue from the boss. He or she will most likely order first or extend that courtesy to a guest. Either way, pay attention. You obviously don't want to order the most expensive item on the menu—nor the cheapest for that matter—so select something in the same price range.

- Don't dig in until everyone at the table has been served.

- If you need to discreetly spit something out (olive pit, fish bone, and so on), pretend to wipe your mouth with your napkin. Others will know what you're doing, of course, but will most likely look away out of courtesy. Also, it's okay to ask the waiter for another napkin if needed.

- Follow up with a thank-you note to the host (see pages 61–63).

8 / Ace Your First Meetings

As you'll soon find out, meetings will become a large part of your career. Even though you probably won't be leading your own meetings for a while, you still have some important responsibilities as an attendee. What are the rules? Read on.

Before the Meeting

- **Understand the meeting's purpose and objectives.** If you don't, now is the time to ask. Always get an agenda if possible.

- **Prepare a list of questions in advance.** More often than not, there will be a point at which the facilitator opens the floor, so come up with a few solid, relevant questions beforehand.

During the Meeting

- **Listen as much as you talk.** If you are reading this book, there's a good chance you'll be the youngest person in the room at most of your business meetings. Since you're still building a reputation, for you meetings should be as much about gaining knowledge, perspective, and insight as about reciting what you know.

- **Bring your project notebook with you, and know it inside out.** If you're called on to provide information, you'll have everything you need in front of you. (See page 33 to learn how to create a top-notch project notebook.)

- **Always take notes.** Refer to the following chapter for some useful note-taking tips. Also, pay special attention to words or phrases used often or emphatically by clients and superiors—then use that *exact* language in future projects and proposals.

After the Meeting

- **Create a Post-Meeting Report (PMR).** Technically, whoever leads the meeting should produce and distribute this report. However, if she doesn't get around to it in a day or so, take a few minutes to create your own. (See page 131 for a template.) Email your PMR to the meeting leader and tell her she can forward it to the meeting participants at will. Resist the urge to send it directly to the other attendees, as you run the risk of ticking off the meeting leader and confusing everyone else.

A final note: If your PMR gets circulated, don't expect a ticker tape parade in your honor. You may or may not be acknowledged as the source of the document. If you don't receive credit, try not to feel as though your efforts are going unnoticed. You've earned a point in the leader's book by voluntarily pitching in when help was needed.

9 / The Trick to Taking Notes

You will most likely participate in thousands of meetings in your career, most of which will require you to take notes. Here's how to keep up:

1. Create your own symbols that designate a to-do item, a shelved item, an item that requires follow-up by you or someone else, and so on.

2. Right before the meeting, open to a fresh sheet in your notepad and draw a line down the left side of the page about an inch from the edge (many notepads come with this margin already marked).

3. During the meeting, put your symbols in the left margin as needed.

4. The *minute* the meeting is over, transfer your tasks from your notes to your calendar or to-do list. Not only will this save you from letting important to-dos slip through the cracks, but you won't waste any time combing through your notes repeatedly to make sure you got everything.

SHORTHAND 101

Here are some of our favorite symbols and abbreviations
for faster note taking:

b/f = before	b/t = between
b/c = because	& or + = and
@ = at	w/ = with
w/o = without	w/in = within
/ = per	e.g. or ex. = for example
esp. = especially	diff. = difference
↑ = increase	≈ = approximately
↓ = decrease	∴ = therefore
→ = leads to	mtg = meeting
△ = change	dl = deadline
c = circa	$%*#! = missed deadline

10 / Get the Worm

Let's say your workday begins, by policy, at 8:30 A.M. You'll probably find that 85 percent of your coworkers arrive between 8:15 and 8:40. Now, if you are at your desk *before* 8:00 A.M. (assuming there are others at the office who will see you there), you will suddenly find yourself taken more seriously as a professional. Why? Because perception is reality. We are conditioned to judge people on when they *arrive* at work and to attribute an extra measure of credit to early birds.

That said, the opposite does not hold true. If your workday ends at 5:00 P.M., it won't matter if you work until midnight— the same 85 percent of your colleagues will have gone home by 5:30. Wax on about how you pulled an all-nighter at the office, and no one will think you're more dedicated. They'll just think you can't manage your time well.

II / Gen What?

Every generation gets stereotyped by the ones that came before. For some reason, people like to compartmentalize the nation's youth—placing everyone in the same tidy package, then standing back and proclaiming, "*This* is what you are."

The theory goes that most of us develop our core values between the ages of seventeen and twenty-three—generally a period in which we bridge the gap between adolescence and adulthood, and begin to sort out our own opinions of the world. Consequently, it's become routine to judge each group by events that happened during these formative years.

As you embark on your first postcollege job, you should be aware of the general impressions that management and some colleagues have of your generation. If you were born between 1980 and 1992, you are considered part of the "Entitlement Generation," also known as "millennials" and "Gen Y."

The assumption is that you've had it easier than generations past, that you've been surrounded by hovering parents and media messages that glamorize reward without sacrifice. A quick web search will unearth scores of articles and quotes from managers who claim they are shocked by the wave of new professionals who enter the workforce and feel entitled to the perks others have earned over the course of fifteen years or more. Here's what they may be thinking:

- You want the glory without the sacrifice.
- You demand instant gratification.
- You resent being expected to do grunt work.
- You can't be bothered with company loyalty.
- You want to be CEO N.O.W.

- You won't do the work without knowing the "why." (Unlike past generations, who accepted assigned tasks at face value, no questions asked.)

None of these assumptions will necessarily be held against you, and collectively they no more describe everyone in Gen Y than the label "cynical slacker" described everyone in Gen X. The point is to be aware that some of your new colleagues will assume you carry one or more of these attitudes. So the sooner you can demonstrate a genuine capacity for hard work and willingness to pay your dues, the sooner you will stand out as a newbie to watch.

Be Open to Learning—Even If You Already Have Some Experience Under Your Belt

The morning after I graduated from college, I started my first real, full-time newspaper job as an editor. I had a lot of responsibility for someone fresh out of the box, so to say I was "baptized by fire" is an understatement. Though I'd already had some newspaper experience by this point (four years at a college daily plus two summer internships), I foolishly ignored the fact that I still had much to learn. My rookie mistake? Thinking I didn't need help and that I didn't need to ask questions. Had I taken some time to understand my surroundings, I would have learned that just because I was used to doing things a certain way didn't mean it was gospel. Had I not come in with an attitude of, "I graduated at the top of my class, what do *you* know?" I may have been more inclined to ask questions.

When I finally opened my mind, I was able to learn. I was able to take away lessons from people who had been in this industry longer than I had been alive, and I felt more comfortable saying, "I'm sorry, I'm not sure what you mean. How should I do this?" I think when you close yourself off to learning, you hit your ceiling. I would have hated to have hit my ceiling in my first month on the job.

Jacque Bland
Features editor, *The Washington Examiner*
Washington, D.C.

12 / Put on Your Game Face

We talk a great deal about professionalism in this book. But let's face it: We aren't robots. We have feelings and emotions. Ups and downs, right? Since we are only human, how do we prevent these from affecting our daily performance at work? Allow us to introduce you to the game face. Your game face incorporates the Four *P*'s:

- **Poised**—You display an unflappable look that reflects an equivalent mind-set.
- **Positive**—Your body language and outlook are upbeat.
- **Polite**—You are always friendly and respectful to others.
- **Productive**—You are actively focused and pursuing your tasks for the day.

Though you may be upset about something in your personal life—your landlord is raising the rent *again*, your car is making a very strange noise, you're worried about your dog's surgery—you don't let it show. You are a professional and understand that you have a job to do and a chain of colleagues and clients who are counting on you to get it done.

So how can anyone maintain a game face on the outside when there's chaos on the inside? It involves a simple ritual: Go to the entrance of your office. Find an empty space on the wall near the front door. Actually, that patch of wall is not bare at all. Really, it's not. It's home to a big brass hook.

And every day from now on, as you make your way into the office, imagine hanging your worries, personal problems, and bad moods on that hook. Immediately after you have ditched the personal baggage, your game face appears.

Note: If you're dealing with a very serious problem or situation that you can't just ignore, see pages 105–106.

13 / Write Makes Might

The Good News: For the most part, your days of academic writing (you know, big, hairy compound sentences) are over.

The Bad News: You've just spent the last four years mastering the art of big, hairy compound sentences.

Welcome to the world of business writing. In short, save the flowery language you learned in college for Valentine's Day— this is about stating the facts in the most effective, yet succinct, way possible. By "business writing" we mean the memos, emails, proposals, and the like that are part of day-to-day office life. As these will easily occupy at least 50 percent of your time from now on, it's critical that you know how other people expect you to communicate with them.

According to a study by the National Commission on Writing, *half of all surveyed companies take writing ability into account when making promotion decisions.* What do they look for? In order of preference: accuracy, clarity, proper grammar, and brevity. So spare your readers the unnecessary details or extraneous adjectives and just tell them what they need to know. This means keeping your emails short and sweet, bulleting your facts so readers can find them quickly, and, perhaps most important, compiling all nonurgent questions into one well-orchestrated correspondence instead of six shot-gun approaches. See the following two pages for examples of strong, concise business writing.

Of course, when you're called on to write something more substantial—a newsletter article, a white paper, a market analysis, and so on—you'll be glad you took notes in college.

Email to a Client

Ryan,

We need to get your approval on a couple of things before we move forward with the luncheon:

1. **Newspaper Ad:** The nonprofit rate for a half-page horizontal ad is **$675**. (The same ad is normally $750.) The issue comes out August 31. Would you like me to reserve the space?

2. **Luncheon Location:** Do you think the conference center will work? We need to nail this down ASAP to proceed with catering, transportation, and so on.

3. **Program Inserts:** Do you want to go ahead and order these? If we go to print today or tomorrow, we could conceivably have them here by next Wednesday.

I look forward to hearing from you.

Thanks so much,
Mandy Adams

Email to a Colleague

Stacey,

I spoke with Hope Conner at Braxton Homes and she agreed to host the workshop on Friday, December 5 from 6–8 P.M. Notes from our conversation:

- She will come prepared to do a 20–30 minute presentation on home improvement.
- She has specialty items with their logo that she will bring as well.
- She agreed to the event discount of 40 percent off retail and will charge only for items that have been opened, so there's no wasted money on unused inventory.

Let me know if there's anything else you need on this project.

Best,
Michael

14 / Never Be Afraid to Say "I Don't Know"

Inevitably there will be instances in which you are asked a question and your mind completely blanks out. You can feel your face turn crimson as you tell yourself you *should* know the answer—all of it.

It's certainly human nature to be embarrassed when a gap in your knowledge is exposed; nevertheless, when you truly don't know what to say, resist the temptation to pretend that you do. Ninety percent of business people are inclined to act as if they have the right answer, no matter what the question.

Honesty, however, is a huge differentiator. Simply look people in the eye and say unabashedly and with confidence, "I don't know. Let me find out and get back to you." Then do it. That's all it takes. And in a world chock-full of puffery, that's downright impressive.

15 / The Ultimate Workplace Accessory

. . . is a well-organized binder. Oh, don't act so underwhelmed. Binders are glorious storage units for all things important. In fact, you should create one for each of your big clients and projects. Sample tabs include:

- Correspondence (important internal and external communication filed by date)
- Work plans (see pages 138–139) and timelines (see pages 140–141)
- Budgets (see pages 142–144)
- Meeting reports (see page 131)
- Project debriefings (see pages 152–153)
- Friday Updates (see pages 48–50)
- Copies of client contracts and invoices (if you have access to this information)
- Background data (reports, research, and so on)
- Notes (handwritten notes from client meetings and the like)

Now everything you need will be in one place if the server crashes, you're called to an impromptu account meeting, you just want to impress your friends, or you get hit by a semi-trailer (yep, you can even dazzle your boss posthumously).

16 / Say Good-Bye to Casual Friday

IN MEMORIAM

We regret to inform you that Casual Friday passed away today following an extended illness. It was approximately twenty years old.

In lieu of flowers, new professionals are asked to purchase at least two take-me-seriously suits, a quality briefcase, and good shoes.

Thoughts and prayers go out to fans and relatives of Casual Friday during this very difficult time.

17 / Buy (and Display) These Books

Here's a list of ten books every new professional should own. Some of them are business classics and others are innovative new works. *All* of them, however, will give you wisdom beyond your years. So don't just check them out of the library. Buy your own copies and study, highlight, showcase, and refer to them again and again and again.

1. *The Brand You 50: Fifty Ways to Transform Yourself from an "Employee" into a Brand That Shouts Distinction, Commitment, and Passion!* by Tom Peters (Alfred A. Knopf, 1999)

2. *First, Break All the Rules* by Marcus Buckingham and Curt Coffman (Simon & Schuster, 1999)

3. *Good to Great* by Jim Collins (HarperCollins, 2001)

4. *How to Win Friends and Influence People* by Dale Carnegie (Simon & Schuster, 1981)

5. *Leadership Is an Art* by Max De Pree (Doubleday, 2004)

6. *Me 2.0: Build a Powerful Brand to Achieve Career Success* by Dan Schawbel (Kaplan, 2009)

7. *Outliers: The Story of Success* by Malcolm Gladwell (Little, Brown and Company, 2008)

8. *Positioning: The Battle for Your Mind* by Al Ries and Jack Trout (McGraw-Hill, 2001)

9. *Selling the Invisible* by Harry Beckwith (Warner Books, 1997)

10. *The 7 Habits of Highly Effective People* by Stephen R. Covey (Free Press, 2004)

18 / Do More Than You're Paid For

The best way to exceed expectations is to consistently follow a simple rule: Do your best work all the time. When given an assignment, follow through—and then some. Examples of "and then some" include: formatted nicely, completed early, researched in greater depth than required, delivered with a smile, and/or accompanied by a stash of candy the Easter Bunny would envy.

19 / You Put Your *What* on Facebook?

What should you post on Facebook? If you are still in college and have not yet entered the job market, relax and have fun. Post away on Facebook, MySpace, and other social networking sites; you still have a little time to be free, wild, and crazy. But for those of you who are seeking an internship or job or have landed your first job, read on.

We'll keep this simple. There is a context clue in the name: *Face*book. You should mostly post photos of your face. It is not called DrunkenBlackoutbook, Boobbook, or BeerBongbook.

Got it? Keep it clean and keep it to normal, G-rated photos of you. The same goes for your profile photo and status updates. If your favorite activities include "bar hopping," "wet T-shirt contests," or "hazing fraternity pledges," you might be damaging your employability and potential for promotion.

As for Facebook groups, now is an excellent time to quit any groups you've joined that may have seemed snarky, trendy, or comical at the time, but now may appear odious or discriminatory in the eyes of an outsider. In other words, you may want to ditch any of those "Corporate America Sucks" groups.

Will your boss or potential employers actually look at Facebook? You better believe they will—and there are multiple ways to gain access to your updates and profile, even if you have a friends-only view setting. (For instance, if you share a friend with a potential employer, they can see the photo of you doing a keg stand or the snide comments you made to an ex.) This e-snooping phenomenon hasn't quite reached Big Brother–levels, but some companies can be pretty resourceful (read: sneaky).

In short, it's extremely expensive to make a bad hire, so most businesses will exhaust every opportunity or research tool at their disposal to scope you out in advance (social sites, Google, credit authorities, checking in with people who know you, and so on). Certainly prospective employers will conduct standard forms of due diligence before they'll meet with you, grant an interview, or offer you a job—and this will likely include a visit to your Facebook page and a Google search of your name.

So now is the time to clean it up—because if you've left anything behind (or posted a photo of your behind), you can lose a real opportunity to get ahead.

Note: This advice should be applied to your presence not just on Facebook, but on any and all other networking sites: MySpace, Twitter, YouTube, Flickr, and the next big one that comes along!

20 / Dining *al Desko*

It's 11:45 A.M. and your stomach is growling. You run downstairs to the nearby Chinese buffet, where you grab some General Tso's chicken and an egg roll. You hustle back to your desk, where you continue to plow through reports and assignments while plowing through your takeout. In your mind, you are showing ambition and working hard. You are back on task and doing the right thing. Right?

Maybe not. First, when you eat lunch at your desk, you miss several important opportunities, any of which are valuable to your career progression. Think about it. You could be:

- Having lunch with a coworker, getting to know him or her better.

- Having lunch with your boss. Okay, so maybe you weren't invited, but you might try testing the water with a casual, nonpushy, "Hey boss, I'm free for lunch today. Don't know if you're already booked, but I'd love to grab a bite with you."

- Out meeting other young professionals, building your network.

- Dining solo—but at a restaurant or café, where you might run into a client or prospect.

- Getting a much-needed break from your computer screen and allowing your brain to recharge. A brisk walk, fresh air, and change of scene—even if you escape for only a half hour or so—often results in a creative spark or insight that leads to a more productive, efficient afternoon.

The second important perspective from which to examine the dine-at-your-desk phenomenon is the perception of others. What message do you send when you eat wontons at your workstation? While there's a chance you'll be perceived as dedicated, there is also the possibility you will be viewed in a less favorable light. It might send the signal that you can't keep up with your workload or that you are introverted and antisocial. Also, most of your colleagues will assume your workload is still relatively light at this point and isn't *that* insurmountable already.

A word of caution, though: Every office culture is different. It may be the norm for your coworkers to eat on the fly, while banging out work. If that's the case, fine. But be forewarned that dining *al desko* can get you labeled as a loner, dampen your productivity, and quite possibly stink up your entire floor!

21 / Flirting at Work: Yes, No, Maybe?

We all know it's *not* okay to flirt with your colleagues or (of course) your boss, but what exactly constitutes flirting? For starters, let's consider "the look"—that unmistakably non-platonic gaze that says a lot without actually saying anything at all. We've all seen the look a thousand times in the movies: A boy and girl are thrown together by circumstances out of their control. At first they can barely stand one another and then . . . the look. No one has to explain what happens next. The trouble with the look in a work environment is that you may think you're being fun and outgoing, but it could be interpreted more seriously. So it's best to avoid it altogether.

When you're at work, it's also important to be hyperaware of your body language. Lots of women, for example, have a tendency to do things out of nervousness—twirl their hair, laugh excessively, touch their face or neck—that could be mistaken for flirting. As a general rule, if you have to question whether a certain behavior is appropriate, it's probably not.

So is it *ever* acceptable to date a coworker, you ask? While company policies vary (check yours), it's obvious why office romances are so commonplace. Where else can you observe—without actually committing to a date—someone's daily habits, communication style, leadership ability, and interpersonal skills? It's almost too convenient really.

If you're just looking to have some fun and kiss a couple frogs, definitely stay out of the work pond. However, if you've made a legitimate connection with a (single!) colleague, the best course of action is to be very discrete about your relationship in the beginning; in other words, no prolonged coffeepot rendezvous or telltale Facebook updates. Make a pact that if it doesn't work out, no one will be the wiser and you'll both keep your private life private. No drama. No hard feelings. No professional repercussions. A word of caution though: Even the best intentions can go terribly awry when it comes to personal relationships.

However, if you beat the odds and things turn serious (and company policy allows), share your good news tactfully and professionally. As long as you don't let your love life interfere with your productivity, most businesses will politely look the other way.

Interested in a Coworker?
Proceed with Caution

The first week at my first job was packed full of training on how to assist customers over the phone and upsell our online dating service. It wasn't long before I started noticing one of my trainers. It could've been that there was a constant sexual tension in the air because we worked at a dating site or the fact that my trainer was playfully flirting with me, but I was really enjoying my new job.

Eventually, I decided that it wouldn't hurt to see him outside the office as long as no one knew. After all, I thought this was actually going somewhere. So we proceeded to become an item, without letting anyone at work know. Long story short, I was crushed when I found out he was also seeing *another* coworker! As it turned out, she and I became friends over the whole ordeal and the trainer moved on to a new job.

I ended up working at the company for more than a year and a half and observed a lot of intercompany dating, both in secret and openly. One couple was able to turn their relationship into a loving marriage, but most of what I saw didn't end well.

K. Ketchum
Account Manager
Los Angeles, California

22 / Writing a Self-*Memo*

When you are new to a job, especially your first job, you are learning at light speed. With so much information coming at once, it's nearly impossible to avoid letting some of it slip through the cracks. A reasonable retention rate may be fine for most, but as someone whose sights are set on the top echelon of success, this is unacceptable for you. Enter the Self-Memo, or *Memo*. Here's how to get started:

Step One: Create a weekly recap, primarily for your own internal tracking and self-assessment, in which you briefly record the following:

- The date and week number
- Your accomplishments
- Lessons you've learned
- Areas where you could improve
- Your goals for the coming week
- Other relevant notes and insights

Step Two: Commit to the Self-*Memo* process for a minimum of six weeks.

Step Three: Sit back in amazement at how far you've come.

The primary benefit of Self-*Memo*s is straightforward: They help you record and retain important information. The secondary benefit, however, is far more subtle. When your performance evaluation (the annual review) comes up and your boss asks about your progress and accomplishments, you'll be in a position to blow him away. When the opportunity arises during the review meeting, you can casually yet confidently present a binder or folder of *Memos*, which meticulously record your career progression and underscore your commitment to learning and success.

This approach will enable you to make an impact that goes well beyond the standard self-assessment form. Your boss will be impressed. In fact, there's a good chance this will be the first time he's seen someone take such initiative.

23 / Above All, *Care*

No matter what you do,
No matter where you work,
You are in a service business.
That means at the end of the day,
At the end of the line,
Everyone serves someone else.
And that someone should matter to you,
Because they are the reason you can do what you do.
So care about them.
See their problems as opportunities,
Their goals as your goals,
And their staff as your allies.
If you can do that,
You're guaranteed to succeed—
Because, in truth, no one expects you to be the best,
But they do expect you to give your best.
And if they can tell that you care,
That you're genuinely trying,
They will meet you halfway.
And sometimes that's all it takes
To go the distance.

PART TWO

Score Major-League Points When You're Still a Rookie

THE INCREASINGLY FAST PACE of business has left employers little time to cultivate their new hires, leaving you to fend for yourself on the job. Here's how to effectively navigate that transition stage when *everything* is new, but you still need to distinguish yourself as a winner.

24 / One Thing You Should Do Every Friday

Beginning today, start submitting a Friday Update to your boss each week. She probably has not asked you to do this, so she's not expecting it. That's fine. The element of surprise will make you look like a hero.

The Friday Update is a succinct email in bullet-point format, designed to get your boss up to speed—fast. It's simple to create and contains a summary of all that you have done in the last week. You can refer to your Self-Memo (see pages 44–45) as a starting point; just be sure to make any appropriate edits before sending it to your boss. (She probably doesn't have time to read much about the lessons you've learned, so focus on your achievements.)

So what *should* you include in your Friday Update?

1. Accomplishments this week
2. Challenges or stumbling blocks (areas where you need direction or input)
3. Noteworthy opportunities, suggestions, and insights
4. Issues that need your boss's input or approval
5. Your schedule and goals for the coming week

The Friday Update functions to communicate your progress and the status of your current projects and tasks. That's all. It should take only fifteen to twenty minutes to write, but it does require some discipline to do it consistently.

Why is the Friday Update so effective? Think about it this way: Your boss is busy—probably busier than you know. When she reads your weekly email, she is instantly informed and up-to-date, not to mention *impressed* by your organization, initiative, and foresight. Suddenly, keeping track of your progress becomes one less thing she has to worry about. As a result, keeping her on your team is one less thing *you* have to worry about.

Friday Update Sample

From: Ima Newbie
To: Yura Bigwig
Subject: Friday Update, May 14

Hi Yura,

Below is a quick summary of what I've been working on this week. Please let me know if you have any questions or would like to discuss anything further.

Thanks,
Ima

Accomplishments
- Completed the first draft of the CreatePex newsletter.
- Front-page (above the fold) article appeared in *The Journal* on Wesley Bank anniversary. Click here to see the article online.

Challenges
- Carter backed out of brochure project, citing budget reasons.
- Susan from CreatePex hasn't returned any emails or calls (heard she's out of town), which may put us a few days behind in the event schedule.

CONTINUED ON NEXT PAGE

Opportunities, Suggestions, and Insights

- Frame Wesley Bank article and present to client at account meeting?
- Would you like me to update the prospect list for your partner retreat next month?

Issues That Need Your Input

- Can you please call and speak with the CFO of Davis about the new work plan deadlines?
- Who is leading MisMasters presentation? What handouts are needed?

Schedule and Goals for Next Week

- Client presentation to MisMaster on Tuesday (May 18) regarding spring campaign.
- Connect with Susan and obtain approval to cohost their open house.
- Account meeting with Davis crew on Wednesday (May 19).
- Boston market research. I'll have this for your review by next Thursday (May 20).

25 / Beware of Circle Talkers

If you ask someone a question and by the time she's finished answering you've completely forgotten what you asked in the first place, you've got a circle talker in your midst. Warning: circle talkers are a danger to themselves and society at large. If you catch one, first quarantine immediately. Then force offenders to listen to each other as punishment for their digressive verbosity.

To avoid being labeled a circle talker yourself, practice being direct in your speech and steer clear of excessive amounts of unnecessary detail and imagery. Try to get your stories down to two minutes or less. Better yet, speak in sound bites. (The press will love you.)

For instance, no one wants to hear about Nelson—the gray Yorkie with the red collar and the lazy eye that your no-good ex-boyfriend Ron gave you—who ran away this morning, preventing you from finding the blue suit with the matching scarf in a timely fashion, which, in turn, resulted in your being stuck behind the oblivious Sunday driver who made you late to the office, which, incidentally, caused you to miss the big client meeting. They only care that you missed the client meeting. Really, that's all they care about.

So spare everyone the arduous task of politely nodding and smiling while you wax on about nothing of significance. Think linear language. Say it with us: linear language. Refreshing, isn't it? No superfluous details. No fat. Now, go out there and get to the point.

26 / Join Toastmasters

Throughout history, almost without exception, great leaders have always been great communicators. (How can you convince people to follow you if you can't articulate why they should bother?) This is why businesses consistently rank "communication skills" at the top of their wish list for young talent. Unfortunately, many bright, passionate budding professionals would rather eat a dirt sandwich than get up and speak in front of others. If this describes you, consider joining your local Toastmasters.

Toastmasters (www.toastmasters.org) is a communications and leadership development program that allows you to practice and improve your public-speaking skills in an environment *outside* your office. It's one thing you can do for yourself that will profoundly affect your career. How? In short, by giving you the composure that comes with exposure. The more you speak in public, the better you become at speaking in public. And regardless of what you do, if you want to get to the top you have to be comfortable in front of crowds.

So, if piping up at meetings makes your heart pound and your palms sweaty, don't despair—Toastmasters can help iron out those nerves. Here's the drill:

1. You join Toastmasters.

2. You give a series of ten speeches (about five to seven minutes each) in front of your local group.

3. You get a certificate, and Toastmasters sends a glowing letter to your boss.

4. You have the option to move on to an advanced Toastmasters program with specialized tracks: public relations, persuasive speaking, storytelling, and more.

5. You become a more confident professional. And when you apply your newfound presentation skills at work, you'll stand out as "one to watch" earlier than your crowd-shy colleagues.

6. Headhunters and recruiters start harassing you, camping out on your lawn, and offering you five-figure signing bonuses. (Hey, it could happen.)

27 / Thirteen Ways to Raise Your Profile

Have people started to take you seriously around the office yet? If you don't know, ask yourself these questions:

1. Does your boss (or your boss's boss) need prompting to remember your name?
2. Are you still waiting to be given your first serious project or assignment?
3. Do your colleagues barely notice when you walk into the room?

If you answered yes to any of the above, you have a problem. Namely, you're not being memorable enough. You're beige. Vanilla. The professional equivalent of rice cakes. And if you want to turn things around, you've got to get noticed *pronto*.

Fortunately, being memorable is rarely achieved in grand, sweeping acts. Rather, it's accomplished with small, meaningful gestures that build on each other, fostering goodwill over time. So, if you're looking to give yourself a little status augmentation at work, consider the following strategies.

I. Prove You Have What It Takes

To stand out, you have to do the homework (read: the hard work) that precedes talent. No exceptions. If this means you have to forgo the latest celebrity reality show to finalize the Hinkley project, so be it. If it means you have to come in early to keep up with your newsweeklies and trade journals, so be it. There are all sorts of gimmicks you can use to get noticed, but sustainable success requires the goods to back it up.

2. Polish and Project Your Image

Think social networking sites are just for your buddies? No way. Use your online profiles and updates to stay in touch with contacts, promote causes you care about, make insightful observations, direct people to useful articles, and so on. Never gripe about anything online and remember that it's your job to ensure that when people Google you, they find material that reinforces the up-and-coming-leader image you want to project.

3. Mind Your Manners

What thoughts or reactions do you imagine people have when they think about you? If it's something along the lines of "That's the #@$*% who always leaves his dishes in the sink!" getting them to remember your *ideas* is going to be tough. This is where a bit of workplace etiquette comes in. A lot of new-bies never go out of their way to do the little things (refilling the paper tray, knocking instead of barging in, standing when being introduced to someone new, and so on), but *everyone* appreciates the ones who do.

4. Be More Than Meat in the Seat

Get to know what's going on in the lives of your colleagues and clients *outside* of work. What are their interests and hobbies? What are their kids' names? Where did they grow up? Are they dog people or cat people?

Similarly, let your coworkers get to know *you*. Make it easier for them to start a conversation with you by having a few personal artifacts on display in your cubicle or office. We mentioned books previously (see page 35), but what about a framed photo of you playing soccer, standing in front of the ruins at Machu Picchu, or fist-pumping Obama? Whatever provides a glimpse into your hobbies and interests is encouraged, but don't go overboard. (If it requires a carpenter, it's too much.)

5. Anticipate What Your Boss or Clients Will Need *Next*

Take the time to outline concept ideas for upcoming projects in advance. You'll look well prepared and show that you are thinking ahead. Plus, you'll already have a jump on the work. Speed is one of the best advantages in business.

6. Emulate the Best

Identify the most respected people in your office and observe them closely. How do they treat others? How do they react in a crisis? How do they carry themselves? What traits do they cultivate that contribute to their success? Incorporate the effective habits and attributes of your company's best leaders into your own work and interactions.

7. Admit When You've Screwed Up

You have the right to make mistakes. You do not have the right to hide them. First, admitting your error lets people know that you know you blew it; second, your effort to learn from it and make amends will not only strengthen your business skills, but also earn you respect, trust, and gratitude from colleagues who may be used to other newbies ducking responsibility for their goofs.

8. Respond to All Email and Phone Messages within Twenty-Four Hours

Your prompt responsiveness will be highly appreciated, even if the only thing you have to say is "I don't have an answer for you right now, but I'm working on it." Remember: Old messages are like rotting garbage—the longer they sit, the more they smell.

9. Start a Collection of Business Books and Keep Them on Display

See page 35 for ten titles that should be on *every* professional's shelf. The reward for this is twofold: First and foremost, the insight you'll gain from reading them will profoundly benefit your career and help you avoid a lot of rookie pitfalls. Second, people can use the books to initiate conversations with you. For example, say the chairman of your company is in town and making the rounds of introductions. Accustomed to seeing the usual candy jars and personal photos, he comes to your desk and notices one of his favorite business titles. Not only will you make a stellar first impression, you'll immediately establish some common ground that could lead to a longer discussion.

Warning: If you can't articulately summarize the main points of your "show horses," don't put them out. This trick could easily backfire if you haven't read the books you're proudly displaying.

10. Subscribe to Leading Business Periodicals

Read notable magazines like *Business Week* and *Fast Company* cover to cover and keep a few back issues in your office. For bonus points, store relevant articles in a binder for quick reference and send the online link to others in your network who might find them useful.

11. Buy the Best Suits and Accessories You Can Afford

How you treat yourself lets others know how they can treat you. Therefore, if you dress and act like a powerful professional, you'll find that people will treat you like one.

12. Keep "To-Learn" Lists

Create a list of five things you'll need to know to move up (for instance, learn Excel, web design, or copy writing) and take the initiative to master each one. When you're finished, create a new list.

13. Be a Freak about Etails

Etails are email details that can get you in trouble if you're not careful. Therefore, always read every email you've composed in its entirety *before* you hit Send. Make sure your spell check is on, that you aren't using abbreviated texting language, and that you are giving the recipient enough information to move the ball up the field.

Don't Trust Technology to Get It Right *All* the Time

I was working for an international floor-covering company and planning to ship new product displays to each regional warehouse. I trusted spell check to correct any typos in my memo, which I was sending to every branch in the United States. Well, what every branch received from me was a memo that said, "Please keep an eye out for these new exciting displays arriving in your local whorehouse in the coming weeks. Sincerely, Tonia." Apparently, when I misspelled *warehouse* as *wharehouse*, spell check automatically corrected it to *whorehouse*. The moral of the story? Always proof important letters the old-fashioned way instead of relying on the ease of modern technology.

Tonia F. Speir
Managing partner, CASE Solutions
Myrtle Beach, South Carolina

28 / Turn Grunt Work into Great Work

At this stage in your career, there's really no such thing as grunt work anyway. *Every* task is an opportunity in disguise. So if the boss wants you to drive three hours to deliver a client package, take them some chocolate too. Or if your supervisor gives you the dreaded task of organizing a room full of filing cabinets, implement a color code system and wow everyone with your creativity.

Even the most mundane tasks—sending faxes, photocopying, shipping packages—can work to your advantage. If you become a fax aficionado, copier connoisseur, and mailroom maven, you'll become a go-to person when someone has a question, a complicated request, or doesn't know where the On button is. So if Sal from sales needs to ship a package overnight to Bangladesh—with delivery confirmation, customs documentation, and cargo insurance—no problem. You can show him the ropes.

For the next twelve months (at least), your mission is to volunteer for the assignments that no one else wants and complete them vastly better than expected. Here's how to get started:

1. List three projects that desperately need attention in your office.

2. Create a plan for tackling each one head-on.

3. Go!

29 / A Note about Thank-You Notes

While email thank-yous are perfectly acceptable, handwritten notes are a dying art. As such, they are more memorable.

If your employer supplies note cards that bear the company logo, use them. If not, go out and buy a box of tasteful blank cards or print your own (high-quality) personalized stationery.

If you're wondering what to write, the only rule is to keep it simple. Twenty to forty well-crafted sincere words is all it takes. Here's a general outline:

1. Thank the person for taking the time to meet with you or help you out.
2. Make a specific reference to your discussion or meeting.
3. Close cordially and attach your business card.
4. Use a *real* postage stamp if you're sending a handwritten note. (FYI: Some studies say stamped mail is *three times* more likely to be read than metered mail.)

Also, when it comes to thank-you notes, err on the side of sending too many rather than too few. Occasions that warrant a personal response include the following:

- A letter of reference
- A job interview
- A referral that resulted in a job interview
- A professional advice or mentoring session
- A testimonial
- An introduction to an important new contact
- An initial meeting with a client
- A meeting with an acquaintance you haven't seen for a while

- A gift
- A coworker goes out of his way to help you
- A training course that your employer paid for
- A vendor or supplier goes the extra mile for you
- A dinner or gathering you attend at a boss or colleague's home
- A promotion

Thank-you notes are truly a golden opportunity to distinguish yourself. In fact, we challenge you to test us on this. Right now, send out at least five thank-yous to contacts within your network. Wait and see what happens.

Sample Thank-Yous

WHEN YOU MAKE A NEW CONTACT

Dean,

It was a pleasure to meet you at the Coleur reception. Good luck with your presentation next week. I hope we have a chance to catch up soon.

Sincerely,
Elizabeth

WHEN A COWORKER DOES YOU A FAVOR

Tom,

Sincere thanks for all of your help on the A&A manual. I really learned a lot from your advice and insight.

Respectfully,
David

WHEN YOU'VE MET WITH A NEW CLIENT

Ann,

Thank you for taking the time to meet with Steve and me today. We really enjoyed the opportunity to learn more about DJG. Looking forward to being part of your team.

Very best regards,
Jim

30 / Make Your Work Look Like a Million Bucks

IT'S ALL IN THE PRESENTATION
Everyone likes to look at beautiful packages, right? So use society's appreciation of aesthetics to your advantage. Take plain, boring documents and turn them into eye-catching pieces that get read.

Change the font, add some color, design new headers. However you choose to spice up your work, the point is to send the message that you take pride in what you do. Even if your business has some strict style standards in place, you can still put your own spin on the design of your deliverables. For example, you can use your logo as a watermark in Word documents or incorporate your company colors into Excel tables.

As long as the end result looks polished and professional, we guarantee you'll find that your boss, your clients—even your peers—will suddenly value the work more, even if the text stays exactly the same.

It's All in the Presentation

EVERYONE LIKES TO LOOK AT beautiful packages, right? So use society's appreciation of aesthetics to your advantage. Take plain, boring documents and turn them into eye-catching pieces that get read.

Change the font, add some color, design new headers.

However you choose to spice up your work, the point is to send the message that you take pride in what you do. Even if your business has some strict style standards in place, you can still put your own spin on the design of your deliverables. For example, you can use your logo as a watermark in Word documents or incorporate your company colors into Excel tables.

As long as the end result looks polished and professional, we guarantee you'll find that your boss, your clients—even your peers—will suddenly value the work more, even if the text stays exactly the same.

31 / Do Feared Things First

Do one thing every day that scares you.
—ELEANOR ROOSEVELT

Missed or postponed deadlines send two messages:

1. I don't really care about this job.
2. Don't trust me with anything significant.

Truth: Neglected deadlines are usually caused by simple procrastination. (Warning signs of procrastination include snacking, calling random people, doodling, updating your Facebook status, "researching"—you get the idea). If you suffer from any of these symptoms, there is a cure.

Namely, do feared things first. Don't put off projects simply because you're overwhelmed or not quite sure where to start. If you need help, ask for it—otherwise, break down big jobs into small tasks and dive in!

What are "feared things"? Feared things are those tasks that require you to step outside your comfort zone. Feared things are hard. Worse, they may force you to perform in areas where you have innate weaknesses.

So be it. In life and in business, you will always encounter projects that are more difficult than you'd like them to be. Don't wait until after lunch, tomorrow, next week, next client meeting—or after you've organized everything on your desk perfectly. Resist the low-hanging fruit and tackle what scares you. Delve into your trickiest, most stubborn, most challenging assignments *first thing in the morning*. Why? Because easy stuff can wait. It's the hard stuff that matters most.

32 / Don't Get Caught Up in Downtime

The nature of business is to ebb and flow, depending on such factors as seasons, trends, and the economy. This is especially true around holidays. You'll notice the phone rings a little less, the halls are a little quieter, and the temptation to check out (literally and figuratively) is a little harder to resist. Most of your colleagues will view these inevitable downtimes as a well-deserved break.

Not you. You know these are perfect opportunities to stand out from the crowd with a little focus, strive, and hustle. How? Here are a few of our ideas:

- Get yourself organized. (Clean up your workspace, delete old emails, file any piles of paperwork, and so on.)
- Check in with clients. ("How is everything going?" "Are you working on any exciting new projects?" "Is there anything we could improve on in the coming weeks?")
- Research market trends.
- Give existing projects 150 percent instead of 110 percent.
- Send clients or colleagues links to online articles that are relevant to their interests or practice area.
- Write an article for publication and get yourself (and your company) out there.
- Send a few handwritten thank-you cards (see pages 61–63), adding some season's greetings if appropriate.

What are your ideas?

33 / Take the Blame and Move On

Blame shifters are rampant in business today. You know, the typographical error wasn't their fault. Nor was the missed deadline or the project that went over budget. In fact, nothing is *ever* their fault.

Don't be part of this club. Blame shifting only serves to divide teams and make you look unprofessional. Accept the fact that you will inevitably make mistakes (many times), but have the confidence to know that your value to the company will outweigh them. Here's how to respond when the going gets tough.

When You Make a Mistake

I. TAKE RESPONSIBILITY, THEN LEARN FROM THE EXPERIENCE

No matter how significant your blunder seems, bigger mistakes have surely been made. So grab your slice of humble pie, make note of what *not* to do in the future, and get back to work.

2. DEAL WITH THOSE YOU'VE AFFECTED FACE-TO-FACE

Don't try to hide behind email by sending your "bad news gram" right before you slide out the door at five. More often than not, you will make the situation worse by allowing it to fester as opposed to defusing it early. As soon as the damage has been done, have the courage to look the other person in the eye, apologize, and ask how you can make things right. Then do it.

3. DON'T GET DEFENSIVE

When you're defensive, it makes others defensive, and there's no moving forward at that point. In other words, you can't shake hands with a clenched fist. (We borrowed that line from Gandhi.) However, if you are mature enough to be vulnerable, you will not only placate your coworkers, you will enhance your own credibility as well. Ironic? Yes. True? Test us.

When a Colleague Makes a Mistake

I. DON'T THROW THE PERSON AT FAULT UNDER THE BUS (FIGURATIVELY OR LITERALLY)

Never admonish someone for making a mistake. He or she *will* seek out opportunities to return the favor, which means you'll lose the ability to make mistakes of your own without retribution.

2. ASK WHY

Before you get too frustrated, assume your colleague was well intentioned. There is usually a very basic explanation behind every mistake. Maybe the person didn't understand the assignment. Maybe deadlines weren't clear enough or your colleague was overwhelmed by other projects. Either way, a simple, nonjudgmental "What happened?" followed by a sympathetic ear might prevent the same mistake from happening again in the future.

3. OFFER TO HELP

Enough said.

34 / Don't Let Your Emotions Hold You Back

People who are unable to control their emotions do not get promotions. Simple as that. So if you feel overwhelmed and are . . .

- On the brink of tears
- Doing a thousand things and none of them well
- Looking for the nearest bridge

Just stop. Take twenty or thirty minutes alone to simmer down, to think, to simply be. Better yet, get out of the office for a while. The projects will still be there when you get back. In the meantime, grab a drink at a coffee shop, take a walk, read a magazine, or practice a little retail therapy. Everyone needs a moment now and then, and it's far better to save face than to lose it in front of your boss and colleagues.

Note: Try not to use this trick more than three or four times per year. Otherwise, you might find yourself permanently at the coffee shop.

Prove That You Can Handle Criticism

I was in my boss's office to discuss an event I'd agreed to organize. He searched his computer for an email and said, "I probably shouldn't tell you this, but . . ." and began to read a message from an attorney who had criticized my work. As my boss continued reading, my bottom lip began to quiver and I actually started to cry. My boss didn't realize it until I gasped too deeply. He looked up suddenly, came out from behind his desk, and patted me awkwardly on the back, saying, "There, there. I thought you would find it as amusing as I did. Everyone knows that guy is a buffoon."

The next time I entered my boss's office I noticed a box of tissues sitting prominently on the corner of his desk. He handled me with kid gloves for a few weeks after, but once I proved I wasn't going to break down into tears every time I received negative feedback, we overcame it. I learned that in the workplace you must have a handle on your emotions if you want to be taken seriously.

Sara A. Pauley
Legal client services manager
Toledo, Ohio

35 / Toot Your Own Horn without Looking Like a Jerk

Since no one likes to listen to the proud musings of the self-congratulatory, it's best if praise comes from third-party sources. Nevertheless, there is a way to go around the system from time to time and pat yourself on the back while still maintaining your humility. For example, say you've just scored big on a project. Here's what you do: Immediately write an email to the entire team, praising everyone for their hard work and guidance. Copy your manager and, if possible, provide a testimonial from the client: "Mary said this was the best retreat they've had in ten years!"

Use this tactic sparingly though—be very selective about when and how often you send an email like the one above. You should, however, always include your noteworthy accomplishments in weekly Friday Updates to your boss (see pages 48–50). If she's aware of your stellar achievements, she probably won't keep the good news to herself.

36 / Keep Your Deadlines Realistic

Here's a little secret that newbies often learn the hard way: It's better to *overestimate* how much time a project will take when you're setting a deadline.

For instance, if you think your research report will take a week to finish, don't announce that you'll have it ready in three days, hoping that imposing a tighter deadline will push you to meet it. While it's tempting to believe that completing the project in less time will impress your boss, you run the risk of *not* finishing on time if the due date is unrealistic. Moreover, asking for an extension will look worse than if you had just built more time into the schedule in the first place. If you tell your boss you'll finish in *two* weeks, you'll give yourself some wiggle room should any unforeseen problems occur—plus, you'll look like a superstar if you deliver it earlier than expected.

37 / Read Ravenously

Make that *voraciously*. It will make you well-rounded and able to hold your own in any company. (A powerful skill, considering how much of big business usually comes down to small talk.) If you don't read, you will be left with only what's in your immediate environment and on television. Slowly but surely, you will lose your edge. Most television is crap anyway. To protest, become a word glutton.

Expose yourself to new concepts, methods, and points of view. It matters more *that* you read and less *what* you read. Newspapers, magazines, thrillers, poetry, travel guides—read it all and more. Regardless of your field or industry, the rewards will far outweigh the effort. For example, say you're in a meeting and the boss asks if you saw the cover of this morning's paper, which had a story about one of your firm's major clients. If you say no, what could have been a bonding moment comes to a screeching halt.

Trade journals are another essential learning opportunity. (If you're *really* ambitious, read your customers' journals as well.) It doesn't matter how difficult your dilemma or how particular your problem—*someone* out there has experienced it, solved it, and written about it. So before your day gets hectic, carve out a block of time first thing in the morning to peruse trade journals or your local paper—even if it means getting to the office ten minutes early, subscribing at home, or sneaking a few minutes to read online.

In short, reading is the single best way to enrich your thinking, broaden your perspective, and stay ahead of the curve. If you don't, prepare to be lapped by others who do.

38 / Don't Miss Your Industry's Best Conferences

Good conferences give you access to heavyweights and rising stars in your field. The best ones leave you ready to change the world.

And that's why we love them. There's amazing energy in a room full of people who all have the same goals. You can't tap into it over the Web, from a book, or on the phone. You have to be in the room to feel it.

Our challenge to you is to find a top conference in your industry right now—and go. Trade journals and professional associations are both excellent resources that usually have helpful information about upcoming events. Ask around your office as well; senior executives have probably attended many of your industry's best conferences and can point you in the right direction. Even if your employer won't cover the expense, consider it an investment in your career and make every effort to go anyway.

While at the conference, try to talk to the featured speakers and tell them your plans. You never know what incredible things can happen when you take a chance. But nothing will happen if you stay home.

PART THREE

Earn Unbridled Respect from Your Boss, Colleagues, and Clients

---

WHEN A NEW HIRE or a promotion doesn't work out, the chief culprit is usually the failure to build strong relationships with coworkers. As a result, your success truly does depend on your ability to work effectively with others. Here's how to stand out by fitting in.

39 / To Get People to Like You, *Like Them*

We can report with certainty (though with no scientific accuracy) that 99.9 percent of the reason people like other people is because of the way liking them makes them feel *about themselves*. Therefore, if you want people to like you, *like them*. Empower them. Make them feel intelligent, valued, respected, and appreciated. Listen to them and take their problems seriously.

Note to the seriously ambitious: Only one-half of leadership is developing the vision for your team. The other half (the harder half) is getting said team rallied around said vision and keeping them motivated. This means effectively navigating the normal ups and downs of work while staying perpetually positive at the same time. It's not easy, but the rewards will be smoother projects, a more cohesive team, and your rising stock as a newbie to watch.

P.S. Seventy-eight percent of statistics are made up on the spot.

40 / Seven Life Lessons in Fifty Words

1. Attitude really is everything.
2. It's twice as valuable to listen as it is to speak.
3. Humor is the great pacifier.
4. Victories are won in inches, not miles.
5. Circumstances are meaningless. It's possibilities that count.
6. Patience takes practice.
7. Accept people for who they are, not who you want them to be.

41 / How to Make Your Boss and Coworkers Hate You

1. Take all of the credit, but none of the blame.
2. Continue to type and/or check your email while they are trying to talk to you.
3. Disregard the pecking order and go around or above them to get things done.
4. Interrupt them in midsentence to make your point.
5. Send rude, heated, or terse emails.
6. Bring problems instead of solutions.
7. Be an office gossip, drama maker, or backstabber.
8. Bother them with trivial nonsense when they're trying to meet a deadline.
9. Be right all the time, no exceptions.
10. Take every opportunity to remind them how busy you are. (Trust us, if you're *that* busy, they'll know.)
11. Let your ego get carried away and forget your role in the office hierarchy.

Know Your Role

I worked for a nonprofit in Chapel Hill, North Carolina, and I was very excited when my boss invited me to help plan the agenda for a statewide training event. One of the skills I had been developing in my job was professional facilitation. It was critical to success in my field, but I had a lot to learn. During the training event, I hungrily watched the more experienced facilitators and thought, "I can do this. I can really do this." In fact, at one point I was so confident that I stood up and started to facilitate some participants on the spot! I was beaming on the inside, sure I was impressing my boss. Oh, I was making an impression all right . . .

My boss took me aside during a break and explained in no uncertain terms that I was not a facilitator at this event and that I had potentially confused people who had come to learn in an organized environment. I went from feeling a hundred feet tall to wishing I could crawl into a hole and never come out. My boss then made sure I understood my job, and welcomed me back into the group.

That experience taught me a lot about keeping my ego in check, knowing what my role is (and isn't) in a given situation, and the earth-moving power of mentoring someone through a mistake.

Elizabeth Damewood Gaucher
Writer and nonprofit executive
Charleston, West Virginia

42 / Embrace Adversity

When most people are faced with a difficult situation, their first reaction is to feel sorry for themselves. They throw up their hands in a proverbial "Why me?!" and sulk about as if the whole world were conspiring against them. Know anyone like that?

Suppose you're an engineer at a large company and a vendor is angry with you. You've purchased Brand X compressors on a project, and the manufacturer's rep for Brand Z, the brand you normally use, has just lost a $5,000 sale. You subsequently hear that an angry mob from Brand Z has gone over your head to your boss in an effort to make you look incompetent. Now what?*

Once a person gets past the emotional reactions to adversity—typically a combination of self-pity, sadness, and anger—they tend to shift into denial: "Maybe if I just ignore the problem, it will eventually go away." Of course, ignored problems don't go away. Avoidance and denial tend to exacerbate the situation, and most problems, if left unattended, only get worse.

The good news is that dealing with difficult situations not only builds character, but also prepares you and toughens you up for future challenges. Think of it this way: With adversity comes opportunity. Perhaps up until this point you have been hoping to be noticed. You've been visibly wrangling for more attention. Well, congratulations. Thanks to the Brand X/Brand Z debacle, the spotlight is all yours. And everyone is watching to see how you will handle this situation. You have two first-response options:

Option A: "Oh, #&$%!"
Option B: "Bring it on!"

The choice is yours, but remember this: *The more responsibility you take on, the more problems you will have to solve.* Therefore, the sooner you can prove to higher-ups that you can remain professional even in crisis mode, the sooner they'll think you're ready for the next step.

---

* The answer is to meet with your boss and suggest inviting the rep from Brand Z to your office so the three of you can have a constructive chat. This will give him the chance to vent his frustrations and give you the opportunity to take him through the purchasing process and the logic behind your decision.

43 / Never Send a Nastygram

The Scorcher, the Howler, the Revenge-Wreaking Rant. It's that "I am nuclear mad at you, and I am going to let you have it" email. The nastygram is the (un)professional equivalent of punching your fist through the wall. It seems to make sense at the time, and it feels really good to lash out. The nastygram has many uses; for instance, telling someone off, expressing anger, setting the record straight, chronicling the stupidity of another, or arguing the case for something deserved that has not yet come to pass.

Example: Danielle's colleague Andy missed a key deadline that caused her to look bad in front of the boss. At first she felt shocked. Then her feelings turned to hurt. After about three hours of stewing, though, Danielle got pissed. So, later that night, she fired up the laptop, sat down, and composed a righteous and pointed message to Andy. She explained, in sharp, acerbic language, how his mistake had cost her credibility, and how (clearly, obviously!) thrown-under-the-bus she felt. Within an hour, Danielle created a true nastygram—heated, witty, and scathing. With a click, it was sent, speeding along the copper and fiber pathways to land squarely in her colleague's in-box.

Had Danielle been smart, she would have understood that it is fine to *write* a nastygram. You just never actually *send* it. Instead, you write it, savor it, admire it—and then delete it. You get all your feelings out, yet no one gets hurt. No relationships are ruined.

But isn't it okay to discuss one's feelings, you ask? Sure, in many instances it is fine to do so. We are not suggesting that you sit back and shut up whenever you've been wronged. You just have to understand what's at stake in the long term. And although most of us are usually crystal clear on our own feelings, rarely do we have *all* the facts and supporting information about any situation in the workplace.

It's on these occasions that you must zoom out a little to understand what you have to gain (which 99 percent of the time does *not* include an undoing of the act or a decision reversal) and what you have to lose. Except in very rare cases, the gain-loss scales will tip dramatically toward "loss" when a nastygram is added to the mix. These losses commonly include loss of respect, loss of future opportunities, and—depending on the situation—loss of your job.

There is a better way. Any instance in which the urge to write a nastygram arises is by nature a delicate, complicated matter. Since raw outrage rarely plays well with management, these situations require diplomatic, skillful communication and a variety of verbal and nonverbal skills. It's important to remember that emails (and text messages) lack emotion and are often misinterpreted. (One study by Silverpop found that email is misinterpreted 51 percent of the time!) So after you have written and deleted your nastygram, if strong emotions linger, take action—but take the high road. Here's a tried-and-true, nine-step solution path:

1. Examine your thoughts and questions—but strive to put personal feelings aside.
2. Calmly and politely request a meeting with the "offending party."
3. At the meeting, briefly express your position in terms of confusion or lack of understanding (not frustration) and ask for clarification. Focus on the *situation* at hand and *not* on the person.
4. Mind your gestures, tone of voice, and eye contact. These things say much more than your words.
5. Listen, listen, and listen some more.
6. Recap aloud what you've heard. You want to make sure that you get it right; plus, this shows that you are listening

in a careful, concerned fashion. "I want to be sure that I've understood this properly, okay? You said _____ [give your recap]. Is that a good assessment?"

7. Express your desire to (clear the air, communicate more effectively, work cohesively, and so on) and ask for guidance on how you might fare better in future situations.

8. Kindly thank them for their time, then get back to work.

9. Let it go. You don't have to love all of your colleagues, but you do have to work together as a team—and harbored negativity is a lose-lose.

YOUR EMAIL MAY BE A NASTYGRAM IF . . .

- You are writing it after 10:00 P.M.
- You were mentally composing it on your way home, during dinner, and during your favorite television show.
- You're so mad you can actually feel your heart pounding.
- Your message incorporates the phrase "I can't believe you _____."
- Any part of your message includes ALL CAPS, pr*f@n!ty, or **boldface phrases followed by triple exclamation points!!!**

Remember: If it's important enough to write, then it's worth a conversation, preferably a face-to-face meeting. Chances are that a nastygram will attest to *your* immaturity and lack of control more than the offense you've so vehemently exposed. So delete your nastygrams. All of them.

No One Wins in E-Warfare

I worked for a *Fortune*-500 insurance company in a very corporate job, and was part of a niche department with only about forty of us on the floor. We worked really well together and became a close-knit "family" with only one problem: our boss. He was causing a negative rift in our family pod. Morale was low, and teammates were dropping off, but no one would voice the real issue. No one wanted to jeopardize their career. So I decided to clear the bad air. I sent a mass email to everyone on our floor, as well as the higher brass across the country that we report to. I explained that the boss was the cause of a negative work environment and needed to be removed.

I stood up and told the truth—I didn't feel bad about that—but I upset a lot of coworkers who didn't want to be on my bandwagon. I got pulled into a lot of closed-door meetings, and our boss was eventually let go, but I decided to leave a few weeks later as well. I realized that I had isolated myself and hurt my chance of advancement at the company because I had established myself as a rule breaker. I learned that in the real work world, you have to follow the chain of command. If you can't talk to your boss, talk to your boss's boss; go as high as you feel the need, but don't claim that everyone shares your opinions—it doesn't make you a hero.

Travis Samson
Co-owner, www.FindFred.com
Columbus, Ohio

44 / The Blatant Change of Topic

Your path to success will be filled with challenges. Mine-fields, puzzles, mysteries, walls, and dead ends are but a few of the roadblocks you will face. But there's another one you should be on the lookout for as well: the sinkhole. Because once you step into a sinkhole, you get sucked into a mire that's far beneath you. What constitutes a sinkhole? Specifi-cally, a sinkhole is any conversation that is inappropriate for the workplace and thus requires a blatant change of topic. This includes coworker gossip, dirty jokes, sexual innuendo, trashing someone behind his or her back, and throwing a col-league under the bus.

Here are a couple of examples.

Scenario #1

Midday conversation at the lunch table. You are preoccupied with a deadline, your turkey panini, and thoughts of getting back to your spreadsheet. Your coworkers Monica and Heather sit down at your table.

MONICA: Have you seen that new guy in IT?

HEATHER: Rob?

MONICA: Yes. I think he's married, but—nice bit of trim in the department, right?

You look up, eyebrow raised, but remain silent.

HEATHER: You're trouble.

MONICA: This morning he helped me carry a crate of copy paper from storage to the printer. I was really close to inventing some M drive malfunction so he'd have to come back to my desk.

HEATHER: You mean *wardrobe* malfunction?

YOU: How about that thunderstorm last night?

Scenario #2

Your office. Late afternoon. You've just finished a project meeting with Dave, an analyst from the finance department. As Dave is gathering his stuff, Dustin (his teammate and golfing buddy) walks by, then ducks back into your doorway for a chat.

DUSTIN: Oh man, have you heard the latest move upstairs?

You begin tapping your pen and clearing your throat, realizing that Dustin is about to start dishing (again) on his boss, Jerry.

DAVE: Oh no. What now?

DUSTIN: Jerry promoted Annelise to senior manager.

DAVE: Tell me you're kidding.

DUSTIN: I wish I were. Annelise couldn't plan her way out of a bag—and now I hear she's the lead on the ISP project. Can you believe it?

YOU: So I heard you guys are going golfing this weekend. Where are you playing?

In each scenario, you wisely spotted a sinkhole and avoided it. Bravo! There was no need to jump in on the gossipy gab about ripped Rob, nor was there any reason to participate in bad-mouthing defenseless Jerry and Annelise. Employing the blatant change of topic, you squelched the unproductive conversations in a professional, nonthreatening manner.

Note that the "blatant" part is a key element in the effectiveness of this tactic. Your retort is so obviously and shamelessly unrelated to the topic of conversation (for example, weather, sports, news) that it throws people for a loop—and that's exactly the point.

If this sounds hard, it's not. The blatant change of topic simply requires a large measure of awareness and a small measure of quick thinking. When you use it often enough, your coworkers—stopped in their tracks—will get the hint. Major leadership points logged on your part (even if they never say so) and perhaps a lesson learned on theirs.

45 / When to Confront a Colleague

If you feel you've been wronged by a coworker, take a moment to ask yourself:

	Yes	No
Do I have all the facts?	☐	☐
Will this matter tomorrow?	☐	☐
Will this matter next week?	☐	☐
Will this matter next year?	☐	☐

Scoring: If you answered no to three or more questions, simmer down. This too shall pass. If you answered yes to all four, refer to the nine-step solution path on pages 85–86.

46 / How to Deal with Difficult Clients

Customers aren't perfect. In fact, they can be downright unreasonable. They can take your work for granted, be stubborn and pushy, and make you want to run screaming into the void. And those are the good ones. In an ideal world, we would each be able to cherry-pick our own clients. They would all be easygoing, think our ideas are brilliant, and pay their bills on time, right?

If you're expecting client service to be this simple, you're going to be disappointed. It's not simple. It's hard, challenging work. It's emails waiting to be answered, phones ringing, deadlines, never-ending questions, and a partridge in a pear tree. On the other hand, it's also extremely rewarding. Because the truth is, there's a gap between where you are right now and where you want to be in your career. And the only thing that will take you to that next level is having clients (that is, the customer) value what you have to offer. The more valuable you are, the better you will be treated.

So don't tiptoe around tough clients; use the opportunity to sharpen your skills and win over even the most daunting, demanding customers. How long will it take before this puppy is sitting in your lap? Two weeks? One month? Mark your calendar, then get down to the "business of whoa." What's that? It's the process of doing at least one thing every day to make your clients step back and say, "Whoa! This kid's got it." These over-and-above details can include a client-version of the Friday Update (see pages 48–50), follow-up calls ("Did you get the shipment? How's it working?"), twenty-four-hour turnaround, and letting customers know when there's an issue *before* it becomes a problem.

Not very many people do these things. In fact, when faced with a difficult client, most switch into either retreat or avoidance mode. Don't be one of them. Don't give Joe Difficult some token e-pleasantries, then stand around the water cooler complaining about what a huge jerk he is. Instead, make it your goal to be such a superstar on Joe's account that the next time your boss asks him how everything's going (and she will), Mr. Difficult will have no other option than to say, "Whoa, that kid's got it."

47 / How to Handle Conflicts with Clients

Problems cannot be solved at the same level of awareness that created them.
—ALBERT EINSTEIN

Fact: You will eventually do something that causes friction with a client, or vice versa. As discussed in previous chapters, conflicts should be handled very carefully and dealt with immediately. Here's a five-step plan that will help you navigate this sticky situation with your dignity and professionalism intact.

I. Don't Ignore the Problem

Again, minor situations have a way of mushrooming into major crises if left to simmer unattended. Therefore, regardless of who is at fault, take initiative and set up a private face-to-face meeting with your client to discuss the issue. (Note: If you've *really* blown it, your boss will need to set up the meeting and be present.)

2. Never, Ever Approach a Client in Anger

If you confront a client when you're still fuming, you may experience short-term satisfaction—but potentially cause long-term (possibly insurmountable) career damage. Chances are no one will remember the crisis in a week, but they *will* remember how you behaved under pressure. Don't try to put out a fire with gasoline.

3. Check Your Emotions at the Door

Focus on the *issue*, not the personalities of those involved. This is "game face" time (see page 28).

4. Briefly Recap Your Understanding of the Problem

Confirm that you and the client are at odds over the same issue. (If you omit this step you might think, for example, that they are upset about the budget when they're *really* steaming over the promotional campaign.)

5. Calmly State Your Side of the Story, Then Listen While They State Theirs

If you find yourself at the receiving end of a verbal firing squad, don't interrupt or become defensive. If you goofed, admit that you were mistaken and apologize sincerely for the error. In truth, all most people usually want is a confirmation that they were wronged and for someone to have the guts to accept the blame. It takes an extraordinary amount of maturity to be humble, but it takes being humble to be great. Remember that.

Now, if the *client* is in the wrong, things obviously get a bit more complicated. It's your boss's place to take the lead on this situation, but it will help to have proper documentation—meeting reports, emails, and such—that prove your case. If it comes down to your word against theirs, ask the client what they would consider a fair resolution to the problem. If it's a solution you can live with, appease them this one time, but keep airtight records from now on.

WARNING SIGNS

If you recognize any of the following tendencies in your clients—don't wait until a blow-up occurs. Start keeping detailed records *immediately* and bring the issue to your boss's attention.

- The client never responds to your requests for additional information, then complains when the project comes in late.

- The client changes their mind multiple times a day, then demands your original quoted price and deadline.

- The client calls at 4:00 P.M., gives you a half-baked idea about a new project, and wants to see it implemented the next day.

- The client makes bad decisions, then blames you when they don't work out.

48 / Protect Yourself against Cynics and Complainers Disease

Cynics and Complainers Disease, also known as CCD, has been tearing through offices worldwide, infecting employees in unprecedented numbers. Those suffering from CCD display an insatiable desire to *talk* about what's wrong instead of *doing something* to make it right. Other symptoms include griping, passing the blame, and seeking new recruits for their downers' guild.

Warning: Colleagues with CCD don't want you to excel, because they fear your actions may cause the balance to tip toward a condition that requires them to do more than they are doing right now. As such, beware of catching this career-limiting disease. Avoid coworkers with pessimistic, obstructionist energy, and excuse yourself from grump-fests disguised as happy-hour revelry. Fortunately, researchers say there is hope: Employees who learn to rid themselves of negative thought patterns have experienced a complete recovery.

49 / Don't Be the Slug

In every office there dwells a "slug." How do slugs earn this distinguished nickname? They do it, you could say, quite effortlessly, by being sluglike in their ability to remain in one place for extended, almost marathon-length periods of time.

For example, say the slug needs to deliver documents to a senior-level executive. Does she get out of her chair, perhaps viewing this transfer as an opportunity to schmooze a bit? No: She sits on her slug tail and waits for her senior colleague to come to her.

And what if she needs to get approval on a project, so as to make a deadline? Does she proactively seek out her supervisor, present her work for approval, and move the project ahead toward completion? No: She sits on her slug tail under the assumption that if the supervisor truly wanted to advance the project, she would have come to the slug's office to obtain the work herself.

Perhaps the slug needs to shift her body position, so as to alleviate the numbness and pain that has settled into her well-rested buttocks. Does she move an inch? No: She sits in the same fixed position, knowing full well that to move at all in any direction could be construed as an energetic gesture— gumption, even—and she simply isn't willing to take that risk.

If you want to avoid gaining a reputation as the office slug, try the following:

1. Remove your hand-prop from under your chin. (Note: If your head falls down, that's a bad sign.)

2. When you need an answer, communicate face-to-face occasionally.

3. When you need to schedule a meeting with one or two peers, get up every so often and ask them (in person) if they're available.

4. Vary your expression. Raise an eyebrow once in a while.

5. When you have materials that need a sign-off, don't wait for the mail clerk to make his rounds or for the approver to come to you. Instead, walk across the office and hand-deliver them.

6. Don't sit in the same position until you can't feel your legs any more.

7. Don't make it your personal mission to know the most about the intercom or IM features in your office.

8. At least twice a week, get your pulse over forty beats per minute.

9. Walk around your office and see whether people recognize you. If they don't, repeat steps 1 through 8.

BENJAMIN FRANKLIN: FOUNDING FATHER, INVENTOR EXTRAORDINAIRE, AND ANTI-SLUG

As a young apprentice, Benjamin Franklin would wheel his heavy load of printing supplies through the streets of Philadelphia, taking long detours that allowed the city's most influential residents to see him. Acutely aware of the power of perception, Franklin took advantage of this opportunity to cultivate his image to great effect. So borrow a tactic from one of history's savviest self-promoters and *let others see you working.*

---

50 / Ten Things Coworkers Want You to Say

Try out these lines when you run into colleagues in the hallway, at the coffeepot, on the elevator, in the cafeteria—wherever. If you deliver them with eye contact and a smile, these verbal pick-me-ups will help you win over new coworkers in no time (just be careful which ones you use in the bathroom).

1. Good morning.
2. Good afternoon.
3. You did a great job on that!
4. Are you free for lunch?
5. Hang in there.
6. You look nice today.
7. I love this place!
8. What's new?
9. I really appreciate the opportunity to learn from you.
10. Is there anything I can help you with?

51 / If Coworkers Are Avoiding You, It Could Be Because . . .

I. You're a Crab

Some fishermen claim that crabs in a box don't need a lid because the minute one goes for the top, another will yank him down. If this describes your general outlook on life, we suggest you report back to the fourth grade. Seriously though, the most extraordinary success—and the mark of a natural leader—comes from helping others around you succeed. Remember, a rising tide lifts all boats.

2. You Won't Shut Up

Being forced to nod and smile whilst trapped in a verbal stream of consciousness is nothing short of torture. If coworkers are generally amicable, but duck and cover to avoid eye contact with you, reduce your oral output by at least one-third.

3. You're a Downer

Misery may love company, but at your company, no one will love you for your misery. Regardless of your past, you have complete control of your future and 100 percent of your life left to enjoy. Choose happiness.

4. You Smell

Supercalifragilisticchronichalitosis. Even just one whiff of it is really quite atrocious. The above *Mary Poppins* spin-off is brought to you by your local peppermints.

5. They're Afraid You'll Ask Them to Do Your Work

Every company has at least one employee who—without authority or reason—simply prefers to dump his work on others rather than do it himself. Don't be that guy. If you're seriously in a jam, it's perfectly fine (and expected) to reach out and ask coworkers to share the load. (Just be prepared to return the favor.) Otherwise, pull your own weight.

6. They Don't Know You Very Well

It's one thing to maintain an aura of professionalism, and it's another to be so walled-off that no one can relate to you. So if the team is headed out on Friday for happy hour, tag along. We've already talked about how you can decorate your work-space in a way that makes it easy for coworkers to initiate a conversation with you (see pages 55–56); that's a great start, but don't always expect people to come to you. Make the rounds in your office once in a while or bring bagels for everyone after a job well done. Whatever your methods, the end result should be a significant improvement in your visibility and in your relation-ships with coworkers. (Believe it or not, work can be fun.)

Don't Be a Stranger in Your Own Office

When I was new to the workplace, I thought the less my colleagues knew about my personal life, the better my work life would be. However, over time, people began to feel uncomfortable around me, shut down, and take it personally that they knew nothing about me other than that I reported to work on time daily, met my deadlines, and always put in overtime.

I still believe that people at work don't need to know *everything* about you, but they do need to know enough so that you seem approachable, trustworthy, and relatable. If your boss and colleagues feel like you're a stranger, be prepared to be treated like one.

L. Hicks
Corporate communications
Chicago, Illinois

52 / Have a Nice Day

There is nothing either good or bad, but thinking makes it so.
—WILLIAM SHAKESPEARE, *Hamlet*

Contrary to popular belief, "bad days" are generally not the result of unfortunate external circumstances (the car breaks down, the client's mad as hell) but rather of internal thought processes (*this really sucks, she's a complete twit*) that lead to self-destructive behaviors. Understand this simple truth and you have the power to change your life forever.

When it comes to misfortunes of the ordinary, it-happens-to-the-best-of-us variety, there's no such thing as a bad day. There is only your *reaction* to the events in your life—which is completely within your control. It all begins in your head. And, with a little practice, it can end there too.

(See the following section for how to cope with more serious, life-changing events.)

53 / What to Do When Personal Tragedy Hits

By now, you know that you have to don your game face at work. You've learned to leave your problems at the door, keep your emotions in check, and put aside any drama in your personal life. But what about those times when you are hit with something dire, possibly tragic or life-altering? Let's say you are sailing through your Tuesday, on top of your game, when you receive an unexpected phone call. You find out a loved one is seriously ill and has been rushed to the hospital. You're shocked. You're upset. You can't concentrate or hide your distress—and understandably so.

Don't try to mask this one. You are human, after all, and bad things can happen to any one of us. So how do you handle this type of situation?

Leave work. Go home or wherever you're needed. You're distraught, distracted, and incapable of being productive. But here's the mark of a true professional: You don't just sprint out the door. Instead you muster up the resolve to compose a short memo or email that summarizes your important tasks for the week and provides updates on your projects. Next, proceed immediately to your supervisor and brief her on your circumstances. You don't need to go into minute details, but tell her enough information to convey the gravity of the situation. Give her your status summary. Then, as a courtesy, request a leave of practical duration (three to four days seems reasonable in this case). She will be impressed with your diligence and understand that you need to attend to your personal emergency.

Depending on your company policy, you may have family leave or "flex" days available, but you may have to use some of your vacation time. Either way, the important thing is to get out of the office as soon as possible. Go take care of your situation.

You shouldn't allow a personal event to compromise your work or your reputation. Conversely, you shouldn't allow your work to compromise your commitment to loved ones when they truly need you.

Bonus points: The next day, if you feel like being a superstar, make a quick check-in phone call to your supervisor. Make sure the things you left behind are being handled. Answer any questions. Thank her for her understanding and support.

54 / How to Handle Your Boss

As a young professional, you may not have a ton of experience dealing with a boss. However, the subtle yet crucial art of boss relations is incredibly important to your success. Here are a few hints about bosses for the new and recent hire.

1. Your boss doesn't really know you or understand you yet.
2. Your boss may feel slightly threatened by you, your ambition, and all of your straight-from-college knowledge and skills.
3. Your boss may have had little (or no) formal training in being a manager or in human resources.
4. Your boss is about forty times busier than you are at this stage.
5. Your boss may have about 1 or 2 percent of his or her time to devote to you.
6. Your boss expects you to understand the fundamentals of your job, but may not have time to teach or train you.
7. Your boss has seen many like you come and go.
8. Your boss may be baffled or mildly annoyed by your "Why this?" or "Why not that?" questions—and may wish that you would just *do* things.
9. Your boss probably has a different communication style than you, perhaps preferring verbal communication (face-to-face or voice mail) over email.

So what's a newbie like you to do? Again, be patient. Give the relationship time to develop. Be careful to avoid being too critical, especially on a personal level. Yes, there are exceptions, but assume that your boss has earned his position through achievement and contribution.

Decide right now to like and appreciate your boss. Regardless of personality, style, gender, or taste, your boss is a valuable resource to you. It is to your advantage to make the most of your relationship by establishing mutual respect and learning as much as you can from him. So set aside any annoyances, perceived shortcomings, or frustrations. You didn't pick your boss—and he may not have picked you. But here you are, regardless. How will you proceed to mutually succeed?

It's important to have realistic expectations. You can begin by understanding that your direct, one-on-one time with your boss is limited (see hints 4 and 5). So make the most of those opportunities by being prepared and focused. You may have to keep a laundry list of discussion topics at the ready for such occasions. Also bear in mind that while your boss wants you to succeed, he's also focused on and responsible for the success of *every other* team member he supervises—in addition to his own success.

Remember, too, that bosses come in all shapes and sizes. Some have strong personalities; others are more low-key. Some may be more extroverted or more introverted. Some are well-versed in hard skills (technology, numbers, or craft) while others are better with the soft stuff (interacting with people). You will probably have more than a dozen bosses in the course of your career. Of that dozen, you may click with half of them, forming a deeper bond. It's likely there will be a few bosses that you feel you barely know. If you are fortunate, you will have two or three great bosses with whom you develop a rich mentor-protégé relationship. The key point is that you will need to relate to and deal effectively with *all* of them.

55 / Things Bosses Love

Let's be clear: This chapter is not about "sucking up." No one likes a suck-up, and frankly, there's almost nothing more pathetic in the world of work. This chapter is about understanding that there are certain things that bosses love—plain and simple.

In business culture, in the relationship between a worker and a boss, there exists a certain set of behaviors and actions that are productive and mutually beneficial. Once you examine the boss's perspective, it's pretty easy to understand why some behaviors work and others flop. The fact is, bosses have responsibilities, often huge in scope, for revenue generation, strategy, and execution. To meet their responsibilities, bosses need certain things. They need information. They need clear channels of communication. They need cooperation. They need to be able to delegate tasks, deliver instructions, and share feedback. They need to be able to anticipate and prepare for what's coming. Above all, bosses need people they can rely on and trust to get jobs done.

Generally speaking, whatever is a good move for the whole team is good for the boss. Bosses like it (very much) when you do your job well—and they love it when you make their life easier. Here are a few other things bosses love:

- **Bosses love to know what you are working on.** Yes, they've told you what to do, but it is comforting to hear (from you) about what's on your desk. It helps them see that you are focused on the right things.

- **Bosses love to know that a task you've been given is complete.** Bosses aren't psychics or mind readers. If you've sent the requested report over to the Plainfield office, let them know or copy them on the email.

- **Bosses love good news.** They get plenty of bad news (and they shield you from most of it, trust us) so a little good news from you can help offset the stress and balance the load.

- **Bosses love learning of bad news sooner, before it gets worse.** Okay, maybe *love* is an overstatement, but bosses *appreciate* when you inform them of an unanticipated challenge or a delay in a project as soon as it emerges. In many cases, the boss can help in ways you cannot anticipate or predict.

- **Bosses love clear communication.** They are über-busy and simply don't have time to read between the lines or slog through pages of tedious diatribe. Say it (or email it) succinctly, and get to the most important items quickly.

- **Bosses love solutions to problems or challenges.** When you approach your boss with a problem (and you'll have to do this a lot), make sure you've taken the time to postulate a couple of possible solutions. Even if your fixes are off the mark, it shows your boss that you care, that you can think ahead, and that you can react calmly under pressure.

- **Bosses love hard workers.** Enough said.

- **Bosses love to know that you are aware of project parameters.** If you are involved in a project, know the objectives, schedule, and budget. This demonstrates that you understand the bigger picture and are aiming for success.

- **Bosses love to hear that you enjoy what you are doing.** Don't fabricate this, but if it's true and you feel it, say so. This shows that you have a positive attitude, and it allows the boss to know that she is maintaining a pleasant, appealing work environment.

- **Bosses love to hear that you've learned something new and valuable.** Your boss may have forgotten that he sent you to Madison for the training course on pivot tables. Or that you have completed a self-study module off the company server. Either way, let him know. Usually a simple email summary will suffice—and you'll earn bonus points if you can go beyond simply reporting progress by articulating *how* to apply what you've learned to benefit the team.

- **Bosses love to be asked for their advice or opinion.** It is good for the boss's ego to know that his advice is still valuable and sought-after. Plus, he knows more than you do. (Use this sparingly. And refer to the chapter opening on sucking up.)

- **Bosses love to hear an informed, insightful question.** Great questions are golden. They enrich learning and show the boss that you are getting it. Example: "You know, I've been reading about the 990 tax form and from what I've seen, is it fair to conclude that when we deal with an out-of-state nonprofit organization, we ought to . . .?"

- **Bosses love to hear an honest, straight up "I don't know."** As mentioned earlier, on page 32, be sure to follow this (every time) with a forthright and affirmative, "But I will find out and get back to you."

- **Bosses love to hear someone volunteer to handle a task.** When you say, "I'd be glad to handle that," the boss sees that you are motivated, eager, and willing to work. Plus, it takes one thing off of his ever-growing to-do list. Make sure, though, that what you're volunteering for is something that's within your skill set and capability, otherwise you might inadvertently step on a land mine.

- **Bosses love new ideas (in moderation).** By sharing a new idea about how your company can improve its operation or work flow, you are showing creativity and perspective. However, such suggestions should be used in moderation and at an appropriate time. In other words, don't try to reinvent the place when you've only been there a few months. You don't have the perspective yet to truly judge the feasibility or impact of your ideas. To boot, you will insult everyone who's been there a while with the intimation that they've been doing it all wrong until you arrived.

- **Bosses love to see their team working well together.** For your boss, there's nothing more gratifying than a high-performing team. Leading a group in which everyone is contributing freely and is engaged in their best role is the ultimate achievement in the management world. While this is not something that you alone can bring to bear, becoming a great team player and relating well to your coworkers is an invaluable skill that will greatly benefit you in the future. So for now, adopt the attitude that you aspire to be part of a great team and pledge to do whatever it takes to help your group get to that point.

56 / Cope with—and Avoid— Workload Overload

Your projects are piled high. Your deadlines are closing in on you. Your desk is a disaster zone. Stress wails like a siren inside your head. This isn't how you envisioned your work style, much less your work life. You're falling further and further behind schedule and can't seem to make any substantial progress. Worse, you can't even carve out time to work on the backlog because new meetings and training sessions keep popping up—and attendance is mandatory. Your head is spinning with questions: *Should I be this busy? Can I ask for help? If I do, will it make me look like I can't handle the work or manage my time?*

Regardless of how you reached this point, it's time to go to your supervisor for guidance—not just for your own sake but for the success of your team as a whole. At this juncture, there are two important things to consider: how to approach your boss and how to avoid getting overloaded in the future.

How to Talk to Your Boss

First off, don't try to handle the issue via email. This is a delicate, important matter that calls for face-to-face communication, so be sure to set up a private meeting. Explain the situation in a calm, factual manner and set aside any guilt or resentment you may be feeling. Essentially, you're doing something that you've probably done many times before—that is, presenting your boss with a problem and seeking her advice.

In truth, bosses *do* care that you are overwhelmed and they're glad to help, assuming you are a hard worker and have already attempted to work through the situation on your own. Most bosses are pretty good at finding solutions, but she will also rightfully expect you to offer some options for solving the issue, so come prepared with a few well-thought-out ideas.

How might the conversation go once you're in the meeting? Here's one option: "Joyce, thanks for meeting with me. I really need your guidance right now. As you know, I'm a hard worker and I think I have a pretty good grasp of my job, but lately I've been in a bit of a bottleneck." Mention the projects that you're currently juggling and briefly describe how you've been putting in extra time and effort to complete them. For example: "Let me tell you what's on my desk right now: The Maxwell report is due tomorrow. The CRM reports are due Friday. I still have work to do on the cost analysis for Sandra. Tim has a proposal he needs me to edit, but I can't get to it because I have to create the presentation materials for the Rockville meeting. I've been working overtime to try to get it all done, but I'm concerned that I will miss important deadlines or let the team down if I don't get some help. Can you see where I'm coming from?" Pause and listen to your boss's response.

At the next opportunity, continue: "I'm sorry to have to pull you into this, but I don't want to disappoint anyone and thought it was time to let you know what's going on. I have some potential solutions in mind but wanted to check with you first about the best way to resolve this."

Now the hardest part is over—you've taken the first step and communicated the problem. At this point, it's your turn to listen carefully to her directions. (If she gives you the opportunity to present your solutions, be ready to articulate them clearly and succinctly.) Take notes and promptly follow up on any specific instructions (handing off assignments, rescheduling deadlines, and so on), then report back on the status of each. Also, assuming the situation is adequately resolved, be sure to express your gratitude to your boss for her assistance.

One final point to keep in mind: The "work overload" conversation should occur very infrequently. If you are having a discussion with higher-ups about this issue more than a couple times a year, you may risk being judged as a weak performer.

How to Prevent Future Overload

Taking care of today's work overload is only half the solution; nonetheless, most people will simply stop there because the immediate fire is put out. As someone who is committed to being a top performer, however, this isn't for you. Below are several strategies that, if followed diligently, will keep you out of trouble in the future.

I. LOOK AHEAD, PLAN AHEAD

The more *specific* you are about how you will spend a given workday—that is, you plan it out in advance according to priority and scheduling—the more effective you will become. For instance, if you know a project is due next Friday, set aside some time today or tomorrow to get the ball rolling, not on the day before (or worse, the day of). Inevitably, there will be some other urgent issue you're called on to complete first, which could throw you off schedule and put you at risk of missing your deadline if you don't get a head start. We often think we need to sit down and tackle a big project all at once. Not so! The best strategy is to segment the action items and work on them a piece at a time over the course of days or weeks.

Another helpful tactic is to schedule a brief meeting with a few peers the day before your project is due. Regardless of whether they're involved with the project, tell them that you would really appreciate their feedback. This is *not* the time to begin tossing around ideas or pulling together an outline; it's the time to review and present the completed assignment. The benefits here are twofold. First, it forces you to get the project done early. Second, you will likely obtain some insightful, constructive comments and suggestions for improvement. Keep these meetings short, focused, and intermittent; remember that your colleagues have their own projects to work on and should not be consulted on every assignment you do. Also, these meetings should occur less and less as you gain experience and confidence, and progress in your position.

2. AVOID OVERPROMISING

Do you typically tend to promise a coworker or client that you can deliver whatever they need tomorrow? Do you frequently put their requests before your own work, even if you have urgent deadlines? You're (understandably) eager to make a positive impression at this stage, but if you habitually create conditions where you have to pull off heroic feats to meet expectations, you're setting yourself up for failure.

When a colleague or client makes a request, get in the habit of inquiring, "What's your deadline?" or "How soon do you need this?" Simply by asking the question, you're giving them the hint that they shouldn't expect an immediate turnaround. Plus, people will usually respond with a reasonable due date when they're put on the spot. If they give you enough time to complete the assignment, the ball is in your court to follow through accordingly. If they *don't* give you enough time, politely tell them you'll do your best but you may need a few extra days or some assistance to meet the tight deadline.

There are two exceptions to the above rule, however. The first is when your boss is the one making the request. In that case, you should respond with a simple "No problem" and rearrange your schedule to promptly accommodate his request. The second exception is when there's a "drop everything that you're doing" project that needs immediate attention. When those situations arise (hopefully rarely), stop what you're working on and pitch in without any griping, even if it means working late or over the weekend.

3. DON'T JUST MEETING-HOP

As you plan your day, allocate sufficient chunks of time for actually *doing* your work. (See page 170 for details.) Try to avoid scheduling days full of back-to-back meetings, especially those in which your presence isn't necessary. (See pages 132–133 for how to minimize unnecessary meetings.) You'll go home exhausted and probably have very little to show for it.

If someone personally invites you to an optional meeting or event (particularly if it's a last-minute request), consider the impact it will have on what's already on your plate. Unless it's your boss asking (in which case you don't really have a choice), respectfully tell the requester that you'd love to attend, but you'll have to pass because you need to meet a deadline or work on some urgent projects.

4. INVOLVE THE TEAM

Many new professionals are inclined to think it's better to do things themselves—rather than collaboratively—so that their talents can shine brightly and they can claim all the credit. However, great team players are far more valuable (and less stressed!) than lone rangers who feel they have to tackle every detail on their own. You obviously shouldn't be pawning off your grunt work, but you shouldn't be working in a silo either. If you're creating the work plan for a project, don't assign yourself to every major task because you think it will raise your profile or because you don't trust anyone else to get it right. Give others an opportunity to share the load *and* the glory.

5. DON'T PROCRASTINATE OR RUMINATE IF THERE'S A PROBLEM

When you find yourself in a true overload situation (as described at the beginning of the chapter), go to your supervisor sooner rather than later. Stewing about the problem won't help at all. Your boss will definitely prefer to hear "This could become an issue if we don't resolve the details now" instead of "We have a major crisis on our hands and need immediate damage control."

57 / Midpoint Check-In

Have you done any of the following yet?

- Participated in at least one outside professional development course or event related to your job? (Learning Annex, Chamber of Commerce, industry conference, and so on)
- Subscribed to your local newspaper, as well as blogs, feeds, or newsletters from leading sources in your field?
- Subscribed to at least one business magazine or industry publication?
- Attended a networking event, such as a young professionals meeting or business after-hours gathering?
- Invited a colleague out to lunch?
- Joined Toastmasters?
- Sent any Friday Updates?
- Sent at least five thank-you notes to clients, potential clients, and/or colleagues?
- Read any of the books listed on page 35?
- Observed any of your company's most successful executives for qualities you could use to enhance your own professional image?
- Purged your Facebook account or other social sites of potentially embarrassing photos, groups, or comments?

If not, what are you waiting for?

PART FOUR
Build Career Mojo

CLIENTS DON'T PAY TOP DOLLAR for average performance. So now is the time to *really* step up your game. To move on to the next level, you have to be able to balance three rings, four plates, and occasionally a ball of fire at the same time. Fortunately, there are ways to avoid getting burned.

58 / How to Land Key Projects

Okay, you've been shining in your work on the small stuff. So why won't your boss give you the *real* projects today?

There are a couple of main reasons. First, you have to earn your manager's trust. If you're new, you are an unproven resource, albeit one with tons of untapped potential. *You* know what you're capable of, but your boss doesn't. Therefore, she's going to test you for a few months or so to see what you're made of.

Actually, *because* you are unproven, giving you an important assignment requires a bit of risk-taking on her part. And until she has a good read on how well you handle the more mundane tasks, she may not be willing to take that risk. After all, her neck is on the line, too, with upper management and probably with the customer as well. Again, patience is key. Go over and above the basic requirements of every task you're given, without expecting the higher-profile projects as a result. Remember, you're still proving yourself at this stage.

The second reason has nothing to do with you. It's about laziness—*her* laziness. Giving a new hire a complex assignment will likely involve supervision, coaching, and answering questions—all of which is extra work on the manager's part. In contrast, it is much easier for your boss to give you the basic, lower-level assignments. While this may be unfair, it is a reality of the workplace.

What to Do

If you have proven yourself repeatedly to your manager on the routine tasks, yet she continues to withhold the more meaningful assignments, you have two options. One is to deal directly with the situation by having a respectful, but candid conversation about your feelings. Don't assume she should be able to sense your ambition; rather, schedule a face-to-face meeting and communicate your eagerness for more challenging work. Offer to take charge of your own accountability. Tell her you will keep track of project review (or "check-in") meetings; you will keep your questions to a minimal, reasonable level; and you will seek help from peers and colleagues whenever possible. Finally, tell her your desire is to deliver a successful project so you *both* look good.

Second, if this strategy does not work, given time and patience, you and your employer may simply be mismatched. If that's the case, it may be time to start preparing to move on. Before you come to this conclusion, however, you should give your present situation at least six months to a year. After that, if there's still no promise of progressing beyond the scut work, take solace. It takes a leap of faith, but sometimes you have to leave a "safe" situation in order to find what you're truly meant to do. Or, as E. M. Forster stated, "We must be willing to let go of the life we have planned, so as to have the life that is waiting for us."

59 / Expect to Be Backstabbed

Have you met a backstabber yet? You will. Some day, when you are least expecting it you will run smack dab into one. Maybe he will be smiling with his arms outstretched in camaraderie. Maybe he's your best friend at work. Perhaps he's somebody you don't even know. In any event, he's around. Sooner or later, *you will get backstabbed.* Yes, it's unfair, but it happens to everyone. Expect it. Deal with it.

Here's how the story usually goes:

1. You've done something valuable, something truly great—or both.
2. The backstabber claims all the credit for #1, possibly even belittling you and/or your work along the way.

Now, you choose your reaction:

Reaction #1

You storm down the hall and into the backstabber's office. You raise your voice. You use the f-dash-dash-dash word. You throw in some finger waggling. And while you're at it, you slam the door on your way out. Then, you head straight for your supervisor's office. You barge in and state your case loudly, passionately, and convincingly, so that your boss understands just how badly you've been wronged. Ignoring his blank stare, you stay until you've made your point. After all, you deserve answers *right now.*

Reaction #2

You take a deep breath and decide this battle is best saved for another day. The topic is bound to come up in a future meeting, in which you will calmly offer up the backstabber as the expert, then leave him to flail about in his own ignorance.

Reaction #3

You compose yourself, shrug your shoulders, and say a silent blessing for the backstabber out of pity. Then, with complete serenity, you walk into the backstabber's office and ask if he has a minute. Assuming he does, you coolly ask him if what you heard was correct and, if so, why he would discount your part of the work. Ask him how things could have been done differently and how he would improve communication in the future. Nothing more is required. If he continues to think the only way to move up is to bring others down, he'll get what is coming to him eventually. Besides, it wasn't your *only* good idea. There are plenty more where that came from.

Turn the page to see the endings. ➔

Ending #1

Congratulations! You've stooped to his level, compromised your professionalism, and really made a spectacle of your stunted maturity. The tally sheet in your boss's head says, *I've got two losers here. One's a backstabber and one's an emotional powder keg. Who should I fire first?*

Ending #2

You took the high road, delaying immediate satisfaction for the sake of your long-term success. Survey says: You're street-smart. Giving the backstabber enough rope to hang himself is a savvy tactic *if* (and only if) handled gracefully and without the obvious appearance of revenge.

Ending #3

You won. Yes, you wanted to make him choke on his own tie, but you kept your game face on. You analyzed the situation and understood that his backstabbing was less about making *you* look bad and more about trying to make *himself* look better. You realize this is a hallmark of insecurity and trust your colleagues will see right through it. You go on with your day, knowing you'll never be completely immune from back-stabbers and deciding to live in a way that—should you become a target again—your character (and your work) will speak for itself.

60 / How to Lead Your Own Meetings

Eventually, you will be called upon to lead a meeting of your own. Here's what you need to know to run the show.

I. Read Up on the Rules

Check out *Robert's Rules of Order* (Da Capo Press, 2004). It's the bastion of meeting protocol. You'll develop a solid understanding of the ground rules and learn the ins and outs of parliamentary procedure, which is often used in formal board meetings.

2. Be Selective about Participants

Make sure attendees are *directly* involved with the project at hand. If peripheral team members are forced to sit through your meeting unnecessarily, they *will* spend the time plotting ways to kill you. Just send them the Post-Meeting Report (see page 131) and let them get on with their day.

3. Create and Circulate an Agenda

Send the agenda to participants at least twenty-four hours in advance. It's not only considerate, but will give everyone time to prepare. To make your meeting as focused and productive as possible, be very specific about what you want to accomplish. Don't just say you want to cover "promotional campaigns"— outline exactly what you want to discuss and what decisions you want to make as a result. Hint: Put your most important items at the top of the agenda to ensure they get addressed before you run out of time. (See the following page for a sample.)

SAMPLE AGENDA

To: Executive Management Team (EMT)
Re: December Meeting Agenda
Date & Time: December 16, 8:30 A.M.–9:30 A.M.
Location: Third floor conference room

Research
1. Internal
   - Who is left to interview?
2. External
   - Review transcript pages and pull quotes
3. Client interviews
   - Overview/analysis of findings
4. Final report deadline

Open House Promotions
1. Flyer
2. E-blast
3. Publicity ideas
4. Any other suggestions?

Vote
1. Budget approval
2. Community service project

Select next meeting date

4. Don't Attempt to Manage Everything Yourself

Depending on the nature of your meeting, you may want to appoint one person to be the official timekeeper and another to be the scribe. This will keep you from being sabotaged by runaway subjects during the meeting and from forgetting key points after.

5. Start on Time, End on Time

Unless it's the client who's running late (whoever writes the checks makes the rules), send a message by starting on time, even if people are missing. Eventually, others will get the message that if you're hosting a meeting, it's going to run like clockwork. (Not a bad reputation to have!) Also, give permission for folks to walk out if you go more than ten minutes over schedule.

6. Facilitate with Enthusiasm

As the leader, everyone will take their cue from your behavior. Therefore you must exhibit the same energy level you expect from your guests.

7. Nurture Egos

Some of the meeting participants may feel that they could (or should) be running your show. Respond by giving everyone recognition, praise, and the opportunity to shine. Remember: Disarm with charm.

8. Engage Your Audience

Always make meetings interactive. You can do this through feedback questions ("What do you think, Amy?") or discussion questions ("What did we do right?" "What could we have done better?"). If you pose a question and no one answers right away, don't be afraid to call on people to get the conversation started.

9. Stay Focused

Though you should always encourage input from everyone, long-winded, irrelevant commentary is as excruciating to sit through as it is derailing to the meeting's progress. So if one of your participants starts rambling out of control, politely make note of their idea for a future meeting, switch the subject back to the task at hand, and listen for a collective exhale from your relieved coworkers. It goes something like this: "Scott, that's great input, but I'm afraid we're short on time and have a lot of items to get through on the agenda. Let's give your idea its fair attention at the next meeting."

10. Provide a Final Recap of Roles and Responsibilities

At the very end of your meeting, take a few minutes to go over what was accomplished and what follow-up tasks have been delegated. Ideally, everyone should leave with jobs to do, as well as a clear understanding of how to get them done and when. This quick summary will keep your team focused on their responsibilities and inform them what others are doing in case they zoned out at some point during the discussion. Also, assuming everyone has their planner or calendar handy, this is a good time to schedule your next meeting.

11. Send a Post-Meeting Report (PMR)

Yep, this is officially on your plate now. See the following chapter for details.

61 / The Best Way to Follow Up After a Meeting

Communication breakdowns are the fastest way to deflate project momentum. Therefore, get everyone on the same page—literally—by creating a Post-Meeting Report (PMR) after every get-together. Here's how it goes:

1. Immediately, while the information is still fresh, take fifteen to twenty minutes to create your one-page PMR.
2. Email the report to everyone who participated in the meeting or needs to be in the loop on what was discussed.
3. Save a hard copy in your client binder.

Your boss, colleagues, and clients may not be expecting this, but rest assured that your organization and dedication to keeping the project on track won't go unnoticed.

POST-MEETING REPORT TEMPLATE

Post-Meeting Report
Re: [State the name of the meeting; for instance, "January Budget Meeting" or "Weekly Team Caucus"]
Date:
From: [Your name]

☐ **Internal**   ☐ **Client:** _____

Attendees: [List who came in order of rank]
Summary: [Write a brief description of what happened]
Action Items:
• [Include a bulleted list of to-dos, persons responsible, and deadlines]

---

62 / How to Minimize Unnecessary Meetings

Some people say that when you die, it's best to die in a meeting, because the transition from life to death will be barely distinguishable. Indeed, there will be times when you're included in meetings that have little to do with your work and are dreadfully—make that *painfully*—boring. Being new, there's really not much you can do about that.

However, an ongoing "meeting culture" that hinders employee productivity is a different story and should certainly be addressed. The key, as always, is how you approach the situation. In most cases, it's best to schedule a brief chat with your boss and politely express concern. (Yes, it's ironic to schedule a meeting to talk about how there are too many meetings, but there is a great risk of your boss misunderstanding your tone here, so this is *not* a situation to handle over email.) Sit down with your boss and, without a hint of insolence, let her know how you're feeling. For example: "Thanks so much for taking the time to meet with me today. I wanted to briefly discuss our procedure regarding meetings. I love that we are all in the loop on the great things that are happening here, and I think our weekly meetings have brought us closer as a team." Then pause and listen to the boss's response.

At the next opportunity, continue: "My concern is that some of the time spent in meetings could be better spent working on client projects, and I don't want to get behind on those assignments." Share an example. Pause and listen, then offer a possible solution: "Again, I'm happy that we have such an inclusive culture, but I wonder if you would be open to establishing an informal meeting protocol? This would help us decide who is critical to the tasks at hand and determine whether a meeting is even needed. I would be happy to send you some additional thoughts to get the ball rolling." Pause, listen, and be prepared to discuss your ideas if she asks you to continue.

Since 93 percent of communication is nonverbal, your boss will pick up on your *demeanor* first and foremost. In other words, if you seem nervous or defensive, it will put her on guard. But if you're open, positive, complimentary of what's *working*, and genuinely trying to improve productivity, a good boss will appreciate the honesty. Remember: Ignoring a problem never makes it go away.

Don't Be Afraid to Speak Up

At my first job, meetings were a very strong part of
the work culture. I spent approximately twenty hours
of my forty-hour work week in them, and as a result
I wasn't nearly as productive as I could have been.
I knew that meetings were often necessary, particularly for team projects, but people scheduled group
meetings even when the issue could have been better
resolved with a phone call, email, or dropping by
a colleague's desk. The meetings also tended to be
overly inclusive—the entire department would attend
a meeting that was relevant for only a small group.

I felt like I couldn't approach my boss about this
issue because she would think that I was criticizing
the corporate culture, didn't value teamwork, or didn't
care what my coworkers were doing. After a while,
I couldn't stand it anymore; I started avoiding meetings just to stay on top of my workload, hoping that no
one would notice. Well, my boss *did* notice—and my
absence made a far more negative impression than
talking to her about my concerns in advance would
have. That experience taught me that when there is
something seriously impeding your productivity and
frustrating you, it's best to find the courage to address
it directly. Otherwise, your resentment will manifest
itself in career-limiting ways.

John N.
Online software development strategist
Silicon Valley, California

63 / How to Write a First-Class Article

It starts out just like any other day. Then the boss knocks on your door and says you've been chosen to write an article on the launch of a new military airplane for the company newsletter. Suddenly you feel the blood draining from your face as you recall the one—no, make that *two*—facts you know about the subject: There is a military. It has some planes.

The upside is that writing an article is as much a *craft* as it is an art, meaning there's a formula to it. Once you discover the formula, you can plug it into any assignment and make it work. The downside is that effective article writing often requires a *lot* of research, which can be time-consuming but is definitely necessary. And while every writer is different, a good rule of thumb is to spend two hours doing research for every one hour of actual writing. Okay, here's the formula.

I. Choose a Topic

This is easy, as it is usually determined by your boss or the client.

Topic: New military airplanes to be built locally.

2. Choose an Angle

Ask yourself the following key questions:

- Who is the audience?
- What do they need/want to know?

PRIMARY AUDIENCE (PI):
REGIONAL BUSINESSES

What they want to know: How to get involved in the production.

Nine times out of ten, you will have more than one audience for any given article. With the military piece, for example, you learn that you're actually writing for three different groups.

SECONDARY AUDIENCE (P2):
PROSPECTS THE CLIENT IS USING THE NEWSLETTER TO ATTRACT

What they want to know: Benefits of getting involved with projects sponsored by the client.

LAST BUT NOT LEAST, TERTIARY AUDIENCE (P3):
CONSTITUENTS OF STATE LEGISLATORS

What they want to know: Government representatives are doing their part to bring new industry to local districts.

3. Do Your Research

Start with the obvious resources—websites, marketing pieces, trade articles—to get a general grasp of the subject. Then go deeper. Is there an expert who would grant you an interview? (If you know she's superbusy, what if you just emailed her a question or two?) Could you ask a few members of your audience what they would like to learn from the article?

Enter everything interesting or relevant (that you can tell so far) into a Word document. Depending on the length of your article, you should have at least three or four pages by now. Next, print out these notes and scan for patterns and themes. What ideas keep surfacing? What are the most important points? You will likely find that sentences that seemed random before are starting to fit together like pieces of a puzzle. At this point, you can go back to the original document and cut and paste the text into groups based on these patterns.

4. Create an Outline

Based on the various needs of your audience(s) and the patterns that have emerged from your research, you should be able to generate an outline like the following at this stage:

I. *Introduction: What is this new aircraft?*

II. *Why is it special/needed?*

III. *How does its production affect local businesses?*

IV. *Conclusion: General recap and future projections.*

Now you can start placing all of your research under the appropriate heading. Some facts and sentences may fit perfectly; others may seem out of place. This is normal. Just create another document called "Extra Notes" (or whatever) to store all of the random bits that don't seem to fit initially but might work later on.

5. Write the First Draft

You know what you're supposed to write about. You have an outline with the corresponding (albeit jumbled) text groupings. Now all you have to do is flesh out the words. Start connecting sentences in a way that makes sense. Add transitions. Link paragraphs. Create a logical flow. This process is somewhat like the paint-by-number books you probably had as a kid. The general picture is clear and you know what color goes where. You just have to fill it in.

6. Revise and Tweak

Naturally, you will do a lot of refining as the article takes shape, but compared to the first five steps this is the easy part. Good luck!

64 / How to Create a Work Plan

Author Napoleon Hill said that your achievements can be no greater than your plans are sound. In other words, if you want to give your projects some much-needed focus (and keep team members on the same page), you've got to have a plan.

A work plan is a list of tasks for a given project arranged by priority and owner. Luckily, it's relatively simple to create: Once you know what needs to be done, when, and by whom, the rest is just formatting.

Sample Work Plan

Herman & Herman New York Launch Work Plan (Phase I)			
Task	Owner	Date	Notes/Questions
WEBSITE			
Completed copy due	SW	1/23	Concept approved. Waiting on client info for home page.
Internal review	SW	1/24	Link will be sent to AS, MJ, & TF on Friday.
Photo shoot	SW	1/30	Photographer's studio already reserved.
Edits due	AS, MJ, KT, NB	2/1	
Copy to client	SW	2/4	Aidan said email is fine; hold on design for now.
DIRECT MAIL (DM)			
Concept brainstorming	NB	2/4	DM ideas must correspond with the website.
Present ideas to client	NB	2/6	
Copy to client	NB	2/8	
Client's revisions due	NB	2/11	
Check PO account	KT	2/11	Do we need to add more $ to the account?
Copy to designer	NB	2/13	
Completed design due	FG	2/18	Are we printing in-house or professionally?
First piece drops	NB	3/2	

2/24 ASSOCIATE TRAINING			
Reserve boardroom	KT	1/24	
Hire caterer	KT	1/30	
Meet with client to discuss objectives	KT	2/6	Discuss at end of DM meeting?
Create media training agenda per client objectives	KT, NB	2/6	COO won't be present for training.
Completed copy for handouts due	KT	2/8	
Handouts to client	KT	2/10	Send to both Aidan and Jill.
Client's revisions due	KT	2/14	
Handouts and executive binder to designer	KT	2/18	Create extra handouts/binder for COO.
Completed design due	FG	2/21	
Mock-up to client	KT	2/22	

TIPS AND HINTS

- Pick a color for each team member and shade their tasks with it. This will help everyone locate their projects quickly.

- For extra buy-in, involve your clients in the development of the work plan. They'll appreciate being in the loop and can often provide valuable insight in the early stages.

- Avoid extra work (not to mention wasted time) by showing clients as much in one sitting as possible.

- Whenever possible, try to pad client deadlines by a few extra days to keep the project on track.

65 / How to Create a Timeline

Timelines are perfect for multi-tiered projects or rollout campaigns. They're concise and easy to read, and they give you the big picture fast. Think of timelines as a chronological overview of the major milestones in your project. While work plans often cover individual responsibilities in detail and include notes, timelines present only the most important deliverables and their projected completion dates.

As a general rule, timelines are for colleagues or clients who need only to scan your project to see that it's on track. Work plans, on the other hand, are for those who are directly involved in the tasks and require a more in-depth perspective. It's best to send both an updated timeline and work plan to the team (and your boss) each week, allowing them to decide for themselves which document they prefer.

Sample Timeline I

Watts Scholarship Foundation Project Timeline	
TASK	**DATE**
Begin audit, interim work.	July 10
Conduct audit fieldwork for the Foundation.	September 1
Hold conference call with CFO on status of work to date.	October 1
Deliver draft of audited financial statements.	October 15
Deliver final Foundation audit report (15 copies).	October 30
Deliver Foundation tax returns (Form 990 and supporting schedules).	November 5

Sample Timeline 2

Krass & Associates
Campaign Timeline (Phases I–III)

Service	Phase I	Phase II	Phase III
PROJECT MANAGEMENT & OUTREACH	Oversee the strategic planning and implementation of the public education campaign. Develop and implement outreach strategies. Solicit buy-in from appropriate community and political leaders. Provide ongoing consultation on deliverables.		
RESEARCH	Conduct bid process and selection of vendors.		
CREATIVE	Develop logo, brochure, advertising concepts (ongoing), website, displays, training video, and incentive recognition certificates.	Announce speakers bureau. Plan and coordinate speakers bureau appearances. Begin media talk show circuit.	Continue media talk show circuit.
MEDIA RELATIONS	Define media relations approach and strategy. Assemble media kits. Select and train spokesperson.	Announce implementation through press release and official kickoff. Distribute media kits to all state media.	Conduct proactive and reactive solicitation of media coverage; e.g., develop story lines, respond to positive and negative attention (ongoing).
ADVERTISING	Plan media buys for campaign based on budget.	Produce selected concepts. Manage ad placements.	Manage ad placements (ongoing).

66 / How to Create a Budget

Putting together a budget sends the message that you can think like a manager when it comes to projects and the larger picture of your company's operations. And though there are as many ways to format a budget as there are businesses that generate them, the following template will get you started.

Sample Budget

Department of Commerce Project Budget		COMMITTED FUNDS	EXPENDITURES		
PROJECT	ITEM		JANUARY	FEBRUARY	MARCH
NEW BROCHURE		$15,500			
	Copy writing		$1,500		
	Art direction			$2,000	
	Photo shoot			$3,300	
	Prepress setup			$500	
	Printing				$6,137
PROSPECT VISITS		$8,000			
	Trade show booth			$1,718	
	Travel				$2,211
ANNUAL REPORT		$6,000			
	Research/planning		$500		
	Copy writing		$1,800		
	Photo permissions		$650		
	Printing			$2,019	
TOTAL		$29,500	$4,450	$9,537	$8,348

Tips for Trouble-Free Budgets

I. DON'T LIST TASKS À LA CARTE IN A PROPOSAL BUDGET

If you do, the client will wind up nitpicking to save money and remove items critical to the success of your project. For example, say you give a prospect the first sample budget below. Don't be surprised if they come back to you claiming that Herb from HR had some copy writing courses in college so they will take over that part of the work. Avoid this scenario by grouping all of the tasks together and costing them out as one unit. If the client still decides the price is too high, at least you will retain some control over what to keep or cut while preserving the overall quality of the job.

Sample Proposal Budget I

PROJECT	DESCRIPTION	COST
New brochure		
	Copy writing	$1,500
	Art direction	$2,000
	Photo shoot	$3,300
	Prepress setup	$500
TOTAL		$7,300 (Price does not include printing)

Sample Proposal Budget 2

PROJECT	COST
New brochure	$15,500
Prospect visits	$8,000
Annual report	$6,000
TOTAL	$29,500

2. GET A CLIENT'S WRITTEN CONSENT TO ANY CHANGES

If the client wants to make a change to the scope of your project that wasn't included in the estimate, get their sign-off on a revised budget *every time*. When you're in the middle of a job and the client switches from apples to oranges (which happens all the time), send them an excerpt of the budget with the changes noted and make sure you have their approval *before* doing any more work. Some companies may require an actual signature while others are fine with email documentation. Either way, the point is to keep everyone on the same page throughout the process and prevent any price disagreements at the end of the job. (Oh, the tales of execs who only wish they hadn't skipped this step.)

Sample Budget Revision

PROJECT	ITEM	COMMITTED FUNDS	EXPENDITURES		
			JANUARY	FEBRUARY	MARCH
ANNUAL REPORT		$6,000			
	Research/planning		$500		
	Copy writing		$1,800		
	~~Photo permissions~~		~~$650~~		
Change order #1	New photo shoot		$1,200		
	Printing			$2,019	
TOTAL		$29,500	~~$4,450~~ $5,000	$9,537	$8,348
CLIENT SIGNATURE: _____			DATE: _____		

67 / Mega Project Management

As a project manager, your goal is to deliver a high-quality service, product, event, or whatever *on time* and *under budget*. If you can do this repeatedly, you will move up quickly. (Think boss inviting you to top client meetings in the near future.) As such, here are some ideas to ponder, steal, analyze, implement, or toss. And though what works for some projects might not work for others, one thing is gospel, regardless: First-class results are *always* the product of first-class methods.

Step One: Clarify Expectations

Before you begin any project, be crystal clear on exactly what is expected. This will save you a lot of unnecessary work and unnecessary grief. When assigned a project, take a few minutes to ask yourself (1) "What do they really want?" and (2) "What can I do that they would not expect?" (It's the unexpected service that people remember most.) You're not looking to solve any problems at this stage, just gather enough information to . . .

SCHEDULE AN ORIENTATION MEETING

The purpose of the orientation meeting is to (1) build relationships with key decision-makers and teammates, and (2) discuss project objectives. Questions you might ask include the following:

- What are we trying to accomplish?
- What problems are we trying to solve?
- What are the obstacles?

- Have we done anything like this in the past? If so, what worked and what didn't?
- What's the budget?

THINK ABOUT CLIENTS' SHORT- AND LONG-TERM GOALS

If you're working with clients, you should also note where they want to be in one year, five years, perhaps even ten years. As you're planning this orientation, remember: People want to know how you can help them make more money and/or operate more effectively. Keep the conversation focused on these issues, and you'll find your meeting will become a lot more productive.

Tip: If appropriate, make new client orientations into an event with great food, gourmet coffee, a token "welcome aboard" gift, and so on. Talk about a stellar first impression!

Step Two: Research

The more information you can gather on the front end, the fewer surprises you'll have as the project progresses. If you're not sure where to start, a SWOT analysis can help you develop a big-picture understanding of an organization and thus point you in the right direction. An acronym for *strengths, weaknesses, opportunities,* and *threats,* a SWOT analysis is a strategic survey, credited to twentieth-century business consultant Albert Humphrey. It's relatively simple to produce and will give you some focus in these early stages. See the following pages for a sample created by a regional young professional's group.

SAMPLE SWOT ANALYSIS

Strengths

- We have excellent support from local communities and businesses.

- We consistently host successful, well-attended events.

- We have a core group of dedicated, proactive workers.

- Our team morale and energy level are high.

Weaknesses

- We have not defined the measurements by which we will grade our success.

- We need to develop an action plan to track events, successes, and new members more efficiently.

- We need to improve our marketing tactics/strategies and expand our media clips.

- We could better articulate why we have chosen a speaker or topic and link it directly back to our mission.

- We need to improve the diversity of the group: job types, ethnicities, industries, and so on.

Opportunities

- We need to identify community leaders (current and aspiring) and get them involved.

- We could gather positive testimonials for use in collateral materials.

- We could work to better engage *all* of the people on our mailing list as opposed to focusing solely on the active members.

CONTINUED ON NEXT PAGE

- We can strive to make additional partnerships in the community and with other businesses.

- There's room to expand our membership diversity.

Threats/Concerns
- There's a perception that the group is exclusive.

- Job loss has caused some of our young talent to leave for careers elsewhere.

- Not everyone is driven by the same goals or values.

A SWOT analysis is an excellent tool for brainstorming creative approaches and solutions with new clients. It can also be used as the framework or springboard for articles, projects, marketing campaigns, proposals, and other documents.

Step Three: Plan

There's a saying that if you aim at nothing, you're guaranteed to hit it. And anyone who's ever launched a project half-cocked will agree that fate has a way of conspiring against you, *unless* you have a clear vision of the end result before you begin. Therefore you need a strategy. But before you can put the wheels in motion, you'll need to know these facts:

- Why are we doing this?
- What are the benchmarks of success? (*Very* important.)
- Who is responsible for what tasks?
- When does this need to be completed?
- How can we do this most effectively?

If you can answer each of these questions, you're ready to create a work plan. (See pages 138–139 for details.) Points to remember:

- Don't get stuck in the planning stage. (Inspirational author H. Jackson Brown dubs this, "Ready . . . aim . . . aim.") Eventually, you'll have to stop planning and start doing.
- Always have a Plan B. (The more projects you manage, the more you realize that if something can go wrong, it probably will.)
- When developing goals for each project, note that they *must* be measurable. This is critical. Otherwise, how will you know whether you've achieved them?
- If you can't explain the purpose of your project on a cocktail napkin, you're not ready to start working!

WHEN PLANS AREN'T GOING AS PLANNED

Try creating weekly or even three-day work plans. This will allow you to analyze what's working and get rid of what isn't—fast.

Step Four: Act

Naturally, a fundamental part of project management is managing the project. This is the action stage. Now that you've oriented, clarified, researched, and planned, it's time to get down to work.

As a newcomer, it's more likely that you'll be managing your own workload than that of a team of colleagues. If this is the case, know that your time to manage a team project will come. For now, it is just as important to manage *yourself* effectively and efficiently. In either situation, the same basic principles apply. Successful project management revolves around four key elements: tracking, prioritizing, producing, and communicating.

TRACKING

Tracking is a basic and crucial, yet often overlooked, part of project management. There are two main steps: (1) checking (and rechecking) the work plan and timeline and (2) being aware of (and meeting) the deadlines. It's important to have both a short- and long-term perspective; that is, determining what's due today, tomorrow, and later this week—and looking ahead to next week and beyond. While everyone looks at plans and schedules at the beginning of a project, top performers look at them daily.

PRIORITIZING

Prioritizing is assessing your tasks and making choices about how to spend your time. Once you have reviewed the work plan, you can figure out your priorities for the day and week ahead. A good approach is to create a weekly to-do list and assign priority levels (urgent, important, optional, and so on) to each item. Once your weekly list is compiled, you can break it down into daily to-do lists and allocate time each day to accomplish your tasks.

A bit of advice: Don't try to cram everything into a Monday. Instead, build a reasonable plan that consists of a balanced workload throughout the week. As you are formulating your daily to-do lists, look at your calendar and make necessary adjustments on days when you have other commitments. (In other words, don't expect to write an entire research report on a day filled with meetings.) If you can't determine what's most important, seek input from a senior teammate or your boss.

There's no shame in asking for help to prioritize your work—
you want to ensure you're focusing on the right things.

It's shocking how little time most people spend organizing
their work in this way. Most jump straight into whatever tasks
look easy or they pick up where they left off the day before.
However, if you learn to manage your time well *now*, you will
reap the benefits throughout your career.

PRODUCING

Producing involves actually doing the work: Crunching the
numbers. Writing the copy. Designing the system. Organizing
the database. Whatever the project may be, a large portion of
time will be spent on production. It is a necessary, often labori-
ous, aspect of any project. In this phase, be sure to proactively
let your teammates and boss know what you are working on
and how you are progressing. This simple act, again, separates
the best from the rest.

COMMUNICATING

As you are engaged in your project, make a habit of sharing information with your teammates and boss. Send Friday
Updates (see pages 48–50) to the entire team and regularly
check in with them, especially those who are providing input
or contributing to the project (face-to-face is usually best here).
For example: "Hey Bill, I wanted to touch base with you about
the Fornley project. It looks like I'll be ready to dive into the
database on Monday. Do you think you'll have the parameters
outlined by then?"

If you are managing the project, make sure to schedule
periodic team meetings. You'll get a feel for how often these
should occur over time. If the meetings drag on into two-hour
affairs, they're too infrequent; if no one has anything new to

say, they're too frequent; if they run thirty minutes or less, you're probably right on track. If you want to confirm that your teammates are on the same page, ask for their feedback. Regardless of whether you're the project leader or a worker bee, learn to appreciate the importance of these team meetings and bring some energy and enthusiasm to the table.

Once you learn to track, prioritize, produce, and communicate your way to success on each and every task, you'll likely find yourself working on—and leading—increasingly important team projects.

Step Five: Debrief

Once the project is complete, make it a habit to gather your team together for one last opportunity for feedback and a sense of closure. Unless the project was extremely comprehensive, debriefings should take no more than fifteen to twenty minutes.

As the project manager, it's your job to tee up the questions, but after that just sit back and *listen*. (Plan to speak no more than 25 percent of the meeting.) Use these internal debriefings to gauge how well you performed as a leader and what you can do, specifically, to improve.

If clients are involved, you should hold two debriefings: an internal one with only your colleagues and an external one with the client and their team. Here are some key questions to consider:

- How would we rate the overall success of this project?
- Did we meet all of our goals and objectives?
- What was our profit?
- Were there any notable successes and/or failures?
- Did we meet our deadlines? Why or why not?

- Were there any problems that should be addressed in future projects?
- What were the most effective practices?
- How well did we work as a team?
- Did we provide top-notch customer service?
- Is there anything we could have done differently or better?

After the meeting(s), create a one-page Debriefing Report—a short recap of the discussion—and share the results with everyone who attended. Note: Pay special attention to the best practices and find a way to incorporate them into future projects. This will help you focus on what's right, eliminate what's not working, and improve your team's overall performance.

Finally, if it was a *really* big project, and you're *really* glad it's over, go out and celebrate after the final debriefing. No clients allowed.

68 / Don't Stop at No

You have this great idea for your office. It's killer. The problem: Your boss is giving you no attention, no airplay whatsoever. Don't worry. It's not about you; it's about him. He's simply too busy to respond to your idea, which probably requires him to think.

If you've been ignored, dismissed, or turned down, it's time to reframe your thinking. Nine times out of ten, overcoming stubborn roadblocks requires not more effort, but a new approach. Most bosses respond to individual opportunity, crises, threats, or profit. So to get an audience for your idea, try this strategy:

1. Do a modest, yet effective amount of research.
2. Present your idea as one of the following:
   - A golden opportunity
   - An impending crisis
   - A big, scary business threat
   - A flowing fountain of profits
3. Assign a specific dollar value to the merits of your idea.

First, Test Your Theory

Begin by conducting a small survey. Identify ten to fifteen people whose opinions matter with respect to your idea. You're looking for a diverse and thoughtful group. Talk to a few good analysts, several folks older than you, a marketing/sales rep or two, a peer, someone in distribution/service/delivery, and at least one oddball outsider.

It doesn't matter how you carry out the survey—paper, email, or verbal—what matters is that you document their reactions, ideas, and suggestions. Here's how it goes:

1. You meet with each of them individually for five to ten minutes.
2. You give a brief narrative of your idea and the problem it would solve.
3. You present a handout that supports and substantiates #2.
4. You ask a few open-ended questions, such as:
   - Does this make sense to you?
   - Do you think this will work?
   - Do you like it?
   - What have I missed or overlooked?
   - How would you present it?
5. You listen and take notes.

At the end of your polling, create a one- or two-page summary to show your boss what others (not just you) think of The Killer Idea.

Next, Dollarize It

Business being business, money always matters. Even if you have the world's greatest solution for increasing efficiency, saving time, or enhancing quality, if the numbers don't work, your idea will get the ax.

Then Take It Upstairs

You have The Killer Idea. You have the dollar value. *And* you have the opinions of others to back you up. Now you're ready to cut through the clutter of your boss's busy office and busy mind. You are armed and dangerously persuasive. Your pitch goes something like this:

Rudy, I have this Killer Idea that will (pick the one that fits):

- Make you look like even more of a genius than you already are.
- Enable you to overcome _____.
- Allow you to avoid _____.
- Increase efficiency/productivity by _____ percent.

This project will generate $_____ of revenue with a return on investment of _____ percent. I've reviewed the idea with X people, including _____, and they agree that this project will work, is feasible, and should be done. When you've had time to review this report, can we sit down and discuss the next steps? How does Friday morning work for you?

69 / You Will Never Be Completely Caught Up

In school most of us had busy periods followed by a period of reprieve. During the downtimes you could catch your breath, blow off some steam, get organized, and regroup. The business world, on the other hand, is a perennial string of to-dos. You can't do everything all at once, so as long as you're giving your best, get over any feelings of shortcoming or guilt.

70 / Plot Your Next Move

You're either determined to make it no matter what—or you're not.
—MADONNA

If the difference between the thousands who make it and the millions who don't could be boiled down to one character trait, it would be this: personal responsibility. That means getting rid of all the excuses (there are no victims at the top!), charting *your own* course for success, and taking 100-percent accountability for your life. Don't wait for your boss, your performance reviews, or sheer fate to dictate what your next position will be or which path to take.

When you expect little, you very often get little. So—right now—*set aside at least twenty minutes each week to plot your next move.* We're not talking about mapping out your whole life here, just deciding on your own terms what *you* want next. Here's how to get started.

Step One: Think about What Interests You

What makes you happy at work? Do you thrive on variety, or do you excel at doing one thing extremely well? What do you like to do when you're *not* working that could be applied to your career? Do you really want to be a senior manager, or would you rather be in product development? It's okay if you don't know exactly what you want just yet—most people don't. What's important is that you stay open to all possibilities. Some jobs may not appear to be the right fit initially, but can actually provide the best opportunities for long-term career development if you give them a chance.

Step Two: Get Your Expectations in Line with Reality

Find out how long someone in your position typically remains in that role. If it's a year, don't look for a promotion in three months. Ask around. How long have other people at your company been in their positions? Questions like these will help in your planning. Note: Execs in small or mid-sized companies tend to be promoted faster. There's far less bureaucracy to go through and, due to limited resources, you wear a lot of hats, which makes you more knowledgeable (read: easier to advance).

Step Three: Survey the Landscape

Find out what opportunities exist in your profession. Ask about job descriptions and specific requirements for each one. What skills are needed? How can you develop those skills?

Step Four: Seek Intelligence from Outside Your Company

Don't limit yourself right out of the gate—the more you know about your industry, the more you can take advantage of its opportunities. Professional and trade associations are terrific starting points. Use them to learn about other jobs in your field and specialized information (like salary data) for each.

Step Five: Develop a Plan

Realistically decide what you want your next position to be. (You can even choose two or three at this point.) Break each one down into a set of tasks and requirements, and start honing those skills for yourself. For example, if you want to become account coordinator in the publicity department, you can take a course in media relations, start learning the local and national assignment editors, and so on—*now*. This will not only help you figure out which move is right for you, but will also place you ahead of the game when you get there.

Sometimes "Small" Opportunities Are Big Ones in Disguise

I interviewed with a software start-up company that seemed like a great fit on paper. When I showed up, they were in a mostly abandoned shopping center in a bad part of town and had card tables for desks. My previous start-up company had lavish offices and all the latest and greatest technology, so I pretty much dismissed these guys and showed little interest in the job. My previous company closed its "lavish" doors, while this other "thrifty" company went on to be wildly successful, with a huge IPO that would have made me very wealthy, in hindsight! There are a hundred metaphors to invoke here, so just pick one—most appropriate, don't judge a book (or an opportunity) by its cover.

Kerry Barnhart
Director of field engineering, Vivismo, Inc.
Pittsburgh, Pennsylvania

PART FIVE

Develop a Killer Edge

YOU HAVE TO GROW YOUR SKILLS to grow your salary. In other words, if you want to *earn more*, you've got to *be better*. There are many characteristics required for winning in business, but none will get you to the top faster than the ones that follow.

71 / You Are CEO of Y.O.U.

Regardless of your profession, you are an entrepreneur and your business is you. What if you actually approached your career this way? For example, you've been passed over for a high-visibility project you were counting on at work. Instead of calling your best friend and moaning about what a jerk your boss is, think about what you would do if you owned a company that had just lost a major sale to a competitor. Rather than waste time whining about it, a smart company would analyze what went wrong, correct the problem, then use what they had learned to land the next deal.

Alternatively, what if you're not really working at work? Say you spend the majority of your days checking email, browsing Facebook, and reactively waiting for your next assignment. As an employee, this might not bother you much, but if you were the CEO it's a different story: No work = no job. When it's your business, there's more at stake.

Starting today, we challenge you to run yourself like a business. That means working like your future depends on it. Because, unless you're Donald Trump, Jr., it does. The next part of this chapter highlights some more quintessential similarities between great companies and great professionals.

They're Invented

Great executives, like great businesses, aren't born, they're made. Successful people create their own lives. They pattern themselves after winners who came before them. They create a vision of where they want to be, then live into that vision as if it were already true. Modern-day examples are endless: Barack Obama, J. K. Rowling, Madonna, Oprah. All come from modest roots. All became icons in their fields.

They're Disciplined

It's been said that to be the best you have to beat the best. And to beat the best, you have to be better, stronger, and faster—which means you have to work smarter, harder, and longer. Think of an Olympic swimmer. In swimming, the difference between gold and silver medals often comes down to a hundredth of a second. (Michael Phelps, anyone?) What if this difference could be attributed to the fact that the winner had the discipline to swim just one more lap per day than his rival?

They're Distinctive

Katharine Hepburn once said, "Show me an actress who isn't a personality and you'll show me a woman who isn't a star." When it comes to making an impression, what you show is what you are, so be careful how you present yourself. Remember: No one pays top dollar for average. Great companies know this and spend a lot of money on image-building. In short, do your best work all the time and do it in a kick-ass suit. Trust us; it works.

They're Focused

The way to achieve your goals in life is to put everything you have into what you want and cut out everything else. Great businesses obviously have a strategic plan to keep them on track. What if you created a business plan for yourself? Like an entrepreneur, think about where you want to be in one year (or five years), set your objectives, and then break each one down into monthly and weekly parts. Note: Initial confusion is okay; wallowing in it is not. So if you're not sure what you really want or what your focus should be, set small objectives and work to achieve them in baby steps. Often, accomplishing little milestones leads to bigger things you never could have planned.

Also, your company may have a baked-in version of this strategy that's referred to as the performance measurement system, professional development plan, skill development plan, personal work plan, or the like. If so, great! If not, don't worry. Just take charge of it yourself. As a courtesy to your boss or supervisor, invite them to counsel you on your personal business plan. Even if they don't have time or ignore your initial offer, put pen to paper and make this happen yourself!

They're Relentless

Think about someone you know who is at the top of his or her game. Chances are this person is always moving, always growing, always concerned with results. There are two subtle, very important factors at work. First, truly successful people consistently use one victory to propel them into another, and another, and another. They can be relied on to get things done. And if it doesn't work the first time, they'll keep at it until it does.

The other factor is that successful people are tireless workers. They love to practice, to train, and to polish their skills. As Malcolm Gladwell points out in *Outliers*, the most successful people in any field typically log ten thousand hours of base-level work (that is, training and practice) before they reach the premier levels of achievement. That's twenty extra hours a week for five hundred weeks. Think of Tiger Woods hitting balls at the driving range after dark, Beyoncé returning to the studio *after* a three-hour concert, or a young Bill Gates pounding out code until the wee hours. Do you have this level of drive and determination? What is the price you are willing to pay to be the best in your business?

72 / Specialize!

Perhaps the most effective way to get noticed sooner is to become known for doing *one* thing better than everyone else. Don't make the mistake of trying to be a jack-of-all-trades. What would really make your company sing? A resident copywriter? A number cruncher extraordinaire? A proposal queen? Find a gap, then start asking for those projects! Before long, *you* will be the go-to person. And if your boss, client, or colleagues need your thing done, they're going to come to you, because no one else can do it as well.

What's your thing?

P.S. Brain surgeons make eight times as much as general practitioners.

73 / Find Your Inner Gene Kelly

Back in the Golden Era of Hollywood, Gene Kelly was considered by many to be the best dancer in the world. With his immaculate choreography and flawless presentation, he was the envy of everyone who saw him float across the stage, ballroom, or movie screen. At the time, there were hundreds of other entertainers who danced, yet none seemed to do so as smoothly as Gene Kelly.

Did he actually float? Nope. Was the dancing really effortless? There's the catch. In reality, it *was* the effort—the very nature of the effort—that made Kelly look so graceful.

Gene Kelly was a student of what we call the "incremental edge." In short, it's the theory that seemingly little acts can make a huge difference in one's competitive advantage. Kelly rehearsed, experimented with, and studied his art to such an extent that he found those things that can only be described as "difference makers." Surprisingly, these weren't necessarily in the motions, mechanics, or movements of dance. More often, the incremental differences were details involving presentation. Kelly's "edge" included the way he wore his hat, the crisp creases in his trousers, and the precisely placed angle of his dance cane. These were the little things that, when taken as a whole, *seemed* to make his dancing effortless.

So today, dig deeply into your profession and discover your own Gene Kelly dance steps. Find those small, incremental, makes-all-the-difference edges in the way you present yourself and your work. How could you improve your reports so that your work stands out as truly great? How might you present a new idea for consideration in such a manner that the presentation refuses to be ignored? (Hint: You need not invent all of your incremental edges from scratch. It is perfectly acceptable—encouraged even—to borrow techniques and methods from others. We won't tell.)

SAMPLE GENE KELLY DANCE STEPS

- Create a unique, engaging voice mail greeting
- Use superb grammar
- Practice impeccable manners
- Send handwritten thank-you notes
- Maintain a consistently polished appearance
- Complete assignments early
- Respond to all phone calls and emails by the end of the day
- Do something special for a coworker or client on occasion (for instance, send a bottle of wine or a gift basket), perhaps during their busiest (most stressful) season
- Give a small gift (like flowers or a favorite business book) to your clients on the anniversary of your partnership
- Buy the best pens and briefcase you can afford
- Carry a business card case and keep it stocked
- Keep your desk spotless at all times
- Know the names of your client's spouse and/or children and ask about them often
- Deliver a bit more than expected on every task
- Make everything you produce look special and valuable
- Think ahead to what your boss or client might request *next* from you and be prepared to discuss it

74 / Make Time for Your Power Hour

Sure, business is about being busy. But there's a certain point at which busy means all you are doing is reacting to the incoming—incoming emails, incoming calls, incoming people.* If you want to make progress on any given day, you have to find time to get things done. You have to find time—actually, you have to *make* time—to be proactive.

Warning: Proactive time will not come to you. This becomes increasingly true as you progress in your role and in your career. The more valuable you are, the more people and tasks will come calling. To a large extent, that is a very good thing. However, it usually means that you are pulled in the direction of being reactive instead of proactive. You will find yourself doing more and more of what *other* people want you to do, and less and less of what you know you truly *need* to do.

Here's a solution that works. And like so many things that work, it's quite basic. Orchestrate; plan; carve out one hour each day that is your time to be productive and proactive. Designate and set aside a particular time slot every day during which you isolate yourself. Turn off your email. Route calls directly into your voice mail. Close the door (if you have one). Call this your "Power Hour" and use the time to crank out projects that really need focused attention. After just one week of diligently following this routine, you may find that you are *finally* able to get on top of the work that matters most.

Note: If you discover that setting aside this time means you have to arrive at the office earlier, so be it. The results will be well worth the sacrifice.

---

* Research suggests the average employee is interrupted at work once every six minutes. Sorry for the interruption.

75 / Cluttered Desk = Cluttered Mind

Here's a quick image experiment: What does your desk look like right now? In the workplace, your desk is an outward sign of procrastination and stress. So if the CEO made a surprise visit to your workspace this minute, what impression would you make? Hint: Two coffee cups + multiple paper piles = not good.

File It After You Pile It

Step One: Collect everything you don't have time to file through the week and place it in a special out-box.

Step Two: Schedule twenty to thirty minutes on Friday to go through said paper mound.

Step Three: Repeat every week.

76 / How to Obtain *Real* Business Insight

If you really want to turn customers into raving fans, take a consultant's approach to their business. This means becoming *way* more than a vendor. It means becoming a strategic *partner* in your client's success. To get started, visit their office and talk to the staff. Read trade journals that pertain to their business; go to their conferences and events. Learn about, and be prepared to discuss, their challenges and opportunities. What are their business objectives? How do they market themselves? Who are they marketing *to*? Who are their competitors? What are these competitors charging for their services?

The Strategic Account Management (SAM) form is a sales and marketing tool that can help you answer the above questions. Moreover, it will enable you to develop a solid understanding of these issues—a quality that will eventually light the path from the kiddie table to the big chair. While you may have little to no direct involvement in sales right now, it's never too early to learn that sales is a strategic process, not some random or mysterious part of business. You'll also notice that it occurs within the context of competition and personal relationships. The SAM form will help you develop key insights about the business world, both in relation to your client's company, your company, and at large, such as:

- Ongoing sales is absolutely vital to the growth and success of any organization.

- A great deal of strategy, planning, and coordination goes into acquiring new business and forming new partnerships.

- It's harder to win new customers than to keep current ones happy.

- Your service line or product division is important, but it's only one part of the larger picture of how your company pursues new business and meets customers' needs.

- A natural tension exists between what the sales team promises and what the operational units of your company can deliver, which is why the sales team may be perceived as exerting pressure on other parts of the business at times.

To get started, see the SAM template below:

STRATEGIC ACCOUNT MANAGEMENT (SAM) FORM

KEY INFORMATION

Customer:

Sector/Type of Business:

Name of Primary Decision Maker:

Principal People of Influence:
- [Owner, vice presidents, purchasing agents, communications director, and so on]
-
-

Client's Services:
-
-
-

CONTINUED ON NEXT PAGE

Important Dates:
- [Annual shareholder meeting, trade shows, client-sponsored events that you should attend, and so on]
-
-

Main Competitors:
-
-
-

Client's Strategic Goals:
Short Term
-
-
-

Long Term
-
-
-

SWOT ANALYSIS

What are your client's strengths versus the competition's?

List ways to demonstrate and leverage these strengths.

1.

2.

3.

What are your client's weaknesses versus the competition's?

List ways to overcome these weaknesses.

1.

2.

3.

What opportunities have been identified for this year?

List action items and tactics to capitalize on these opportunities.

1.

2.

3.

What types of threats is your client facing?

List specific strategies to deal with these threats.

1.

2.

3.

77 / Connect the Dots

Big ideas come from the unconscious.
    —DAVID OGILVY, *advertising legend*

People who can simultaneously hold multiple ideas, concepts, and questions in their minds while working on day-to-day tasks have the power of peripheral vision. While others see random, unrelated events, those with peripheral vision see patterns forming, and as a result, they are able to spot trends sooner than most.

Those who focus straight ahead—on only what's directly in front of them—miss out on the synergy of the creative mind. Sure, they notice seminal events and can postulate cause and effect, but they do so only in a reactive way. In contrast, those who develop their peripheral vision skills gain a valuable competitive advantage.

In business, most of us use our left brain by nature—to crunch numbers, formulate schedules, and carry out tasks that involve a high degree of logic. That's all well and good, but do you know how to tap into your right brain? *This* is the part of your mind that deals with concepts, spatial relationships, images, and patterns—and it's a completely different animal.

Because right-brain thinking is rooted in creativity, tapping into it can be an almost indirect or subconscious process. For some people, the right brain is triggered by repetitive, somewhat mindless, activities—like showering, shaving, long drives in the car, or ironing a shirt. For others, right-brain thinking requires a period of isolation to focus entirely on the task at hand. Regardless of your approach, accessing the right brain often results in a truly unique idea or solution—sometimes even a Newton-like epiphany. (*Aha!*)

So, today, allow your mind (specifically your right brain) to run free. Think about how you can bring some *true* creativity to your workplace, and how you can solve your client's problems with a paintbrush instead of a cookie cutter.

EXTRA-CREDIT ENLIGHTENMENT

For further study on unleashing the power of your right brain, check out two great books on the topic. The first is *Drawing on the Right Side of the Brain* by Betty Edwards (J. P. Tarcher, 1999); the other is *The Breakout Principle* by Herbert Benson, MD, and William Proctor (Scribner, 2003). These books will change the way you view the world *and* the work you do.

---

78 / Become a Student of the World

Take advantage of every opportunity to travel, particularly abroad. In addition to gaining valuable exposure to new cultures and outlooks, you'll learn a lot about yourself and develop a sophistication that will help your career. Besides, if you don't get out of the office once in a while, you'll become a dreadful bore at parties.

Take Your Career to a Whole New Place with Travel

It's a well-worn cliché to say that travel is as much about self-discovery as it is about discovering the world, but every cliché has a kernel of truth, and travel really can provide a unique confidence, independence, and breadth of experience that is difficult to acquire any other way. Once you've dealt with endless bureaucracy at the Nepalese embassy in Delhi, haggled for a good price at a market in Istanbul, worked out what to do when your wallet is stolen in Mexico City, and (barely) survived a twelve-hour bus ride in Tanzania, you can certainly handle any situation your first job might throw at you.

Of course, there's a good chance that your first job will be in a business that operates internationally, in which case your travel experience may well have more tangible benefits. Swapping stories about your favorite London pubs with a visiting executive from England or offering a colleague your vote for the best pizzeria in Rome could help you make contacts in places you may never have dreamed.

Moreover, travel not only imparts an understanding of how other cultures work, it also allows you to step outside your *own* culture and see it with fresh eyes and a new perspective. For people in innovative or creative industries, this is enormously helpful in generating outside-the-box ideas and challenging the status quo.

continued

Mark Twain said, "Travel is fatal to prejudice, bigotry, and narrow-mindedness." The subtle form of narrow-mindedness that inevitably results from staying in the same place forever is a massive potential handicap to your career. Take every opportunity to go out into the world, discover how others live, and find out more about yourself and your own culture too. There will be days that are so much fun you'll never forget them, and there will probably be days when you're cold, hungry, and homesick, but you can learn as much from the bad times as the good ones. In the end, it will all be worth it, I promise you.

Matt Wall, PhD
Neuroscientist
London, England

79 / Seriously Grow Your Network

The saying "It's not what you know, it's who you know" isn't entirely true, but there's a lot to be said for having friends in the right places. In fact, a sound network will become one of the most (if not *the* most) important business tools you'll ever have. It will help you:

- Get promoted faster
- Solve problems more quickly
- Dodge novice mistakes
- Find additional information and resources
- Acquire new jobs
- Join a club, council, board, or committee
- Avoid cold-calling forever

And that's just the beginning. Your network consists of people you know, people you've met, and—equally important—people you want to meet. To start, compile their contact information in an electronic database (Outlook and most other email programs have them) or any other centralized, easily accessible format. Then, when you have a question or need information, you'll have a number of valuable sources to consult. This will enable you to work better—faster—no matter what the task or challenge. Here are some additional rules for growing a network.

I. Maintain a Complete LinkedIn Profile

LinkedIn has become *the* source for online professional networking. If you're new to the process, visit http://grads.linkedin .com for details. If you already have a LinkedIn account, make sure your profile is 100 percent complete and that you keep it current at all times. The site also has a lot of handy tools that can help you find jobs in your industry, research companies of interest, and connect with professional groups/associations and their members.

2. Update Your Information Religiously

The great thing about sites like LinkedIn is that your contacts update their own information, which keeps it pretty accurate. However, not everyone has an online profile, so it's a good idea to keep your own database of contacts updated as well. Every time you meet a new colleague, customer, vendor, reporter, or someone who simply impresses you as intelligent or valuable, add his or her information to Outlook or whichever program you use.

Tip: Create a file folder labeled "Network" where you store business cards and contact info until you're ready to update your database. This will allow you to take care of everything in one sitting.

3. Give as Much as You Take, If Not More

Be a resource to your contacts as well. Send them interesting articles, clippings, links to useful information, trend-spotting observations—anything you feel might be beneficial to their business pursuits. The secret to successful networking is that when your contacts win, *you* win too (and vice versa). Think about it.

4. Don't Spam Your Contacts' In-Boxes

Never send anyone in your network random forwards, warnings, apocalyptic rumors, or jokes. Period.

5. Put Yourself Out There

Take an active approach to meeting new people and expanding your network. Seek out clubs, nonprofit boards, and associations relevant to your business. Get involved with your local chamber of commerce or young professional's group. Attend your industry's trade shows and hand out cards indiscriminately. (You never know . . .) There are a million ways to grow your contacts, but all of them require you to make the first move.

PART SIX

Become a Skilled, Nontoxic Leader

EXTRAORDINARY ACHIEVEMENT comes from the ability to truly *inspire* people and *motivate* them to do their best work. This is the crossroads where amateurs end and leaders begin.

80 / You'll Never Lead People Who Don't Respect You

Here's a little secret of the business world: Your success depends as much on your *colleagues* as it does on your own talent and abilities. A lot of people enter the workforce thinking it's a competition. They believe that if they're going to get a bigger piece of the pie, then someone else's piece has to be smaller to compensate. Here's the problem with that: Say, for example, that a desirable project manager position opens up, and after vying ruthlessly for the role, you're chosen as the new leader. Now you're in a situation where you must rally and motivate the very same colleagues you stepped on to get the job. Not a great way to begin.

So if you really want to distinguish yourself as a leader, start by earning the trust and confidence of management *and* your colleagues. How? Just roll up your sleeves. People *respect* (key word here) other people who volunteer when there is work to be done and then finish the job quickly and thoroughly— without griping about it and especially without touting their sacrifice. Before long, there will come a time when you are called off the bench to manage a team of your peers. Prove yourself a worthy leader *now* and they will follow you later.

81 / The Leadership Test

Leaders have to learn to manage themselves before they can manage others.

——PETER DRUCKER, *business thought leader*

How do you know whether you're viewed as a leader? Ask yourself the following:

- Do colleagues ever come to you for advice on how to handle tricky situations? (Regardless of whether the issue is personal or professional, what matters is that they trust your opinion.)
- Is your boss gradually giving you more responsibility?
- Have you been assigned any challenging projects in preparation for a bigger role?
- Do colleagues actively seek you out to join their project teams?

All of these are crucial indicators as to how well you are positioning yourself as a potential leader. If you answered no to any of the above and want to boost your leadership profile, try the following strategies.

Step Up Your Game

Before you'll be trusted with additional responsibility and more challenging projects, you have to excel in your current position. So remember that every assignment is a test (even the seemingly little ones) and give 110 percent all the time. See pages 54–58 for some specific ways to raise your profile and present yourself as an up-and-coming professional.

Volunteer in Your Community

Taking charge in a volunteer group is the ultimate test of your effectiveness as a leader because it's all carrot and no stick. Volunteers don't *have* to follow you, so if you're successfully leading in this capacity, these skills will readily translate to the workplace. Volunteering also gives you the chance to make mistakes as you're learning without any ramifications on your real job.

Use Your Social Media Networks

Instead of posting status updates about the awesome grilled cheese you just made, try sharing professional development articles, posing questions related to your industry, or writing about interesting lessons you learned in a recent training event. The more thoughtful and selective you are about what information you put online, the more you will reinforce the executive image you want to project.

Build On (and Show Off) Your Strengths

Create a list of the top three reasons your company's very best employees would want to work for *you*. For example, you have the ability to remain composed and make good decisions under pressure, you have extensive knowledge of a particular industry, you display an interest in their professional success, and so on. Make it your daily mission to showcase and cultivate these strengths, as well as develop new ones, and you'll soon find your leadership stock on the rise.

82 / Avoid Decision Making by Committee

With so many different personalities in one room, the same issues go round and round the table but rarely get resolved. On the other hand, if you're looking for a surefire way to sabotage or delay a project, committees can be beautiful. However, with so many different personalities in one room, the same issues go round and round the table, but rarely get resolved. Conversely, if you're looking for a surefire way to sabotage or delay a project, committees can be beautiful. Having said that, with so many different personalities in one room, the same issues go round and round the table, but rarely get resolved. On the flip side, if you're looking for a surefire way to sabotage or delay a project, committees can be beautiful.

83 / Share the Spotlight

Every once in a while you will find yourself standing alone, basking under the spotlight of glowing praise. When this happens, resist the temptation to enjoy it all by yourself. Instead, share the spotlight. Spread it around a bit. Rare indeed is the occasion when one truly deserves *all* the credit. More often than not, success is the result of a team effort. And nothing takes the starch out of a good team faster than a leader who upstages the supporting cast.

What's that you say? The idea was *yours*? And you did the bulk of the work? Even so, share the credit. In business, there is seldom a role for the lone ranger. Why? First, we presume that you want to become a leader. As such, it is your job to make the *team* look good. True leaders are unselfish. They sacrifice their time in the limelight to reap the rewards of a loyal, motivated team. Second, there will eventually come a time when you are in the corps, playing a finite bit part, in an award-winning production. In that case, you will naturally want to receive credit for your performance—regardless of how small your role.

84 / Let People Learn for Themselves

When advising or supervising colleagues on a challenging project, don't automatically spoon-feed them the solution as you would have done it. Rather, get them to really *think* about the situation. Give the team a clear picture of the desired result and ample time to get it done, and then let them decide how to get there. Along the way, engage them with questions like, "Why do you think the client responded like this?" or "Is there anything we could have done differently?" Most people remember more of what they discover on their own, so gently *guide* your coworkers to the answer if you want them to see the light.

85 / Be Strict about Deadlines

Missing deadlines is one of *the* quickest ways to irritate colleagues and clients. It disrupts their work plans and creates serious project complications. Moreover, if you miss your deadlines, you lose the power to hold others accountable for theirs. If you're in charge, the best way to handle deadlines is to circulate a draft work plan through the account team. Ask everyone if they are able to meet their due dates; then (this is critical) *get their sign-off.* The thought of coming face-to-face with their own signature as documented approval should curb any coworker's excuses ("I didn't know" or "I didn't have enough time") down the road.

How do you handle coworkers who are always late turning in work? For starters, try setting their deadlines at least three days ahead of schedule. (Shhh . . . this trick doesn't work if they know about it.) Next, have your team send you a Friday Update (see pages 48–50) every week so you can chart each member's progress and troubleshoot minor issues before they become major problems.

86 / Give Back

What causes do you care about? Homelessness? The arts?
Domestic violence? Literacy? Finding a cure for Alzheimer's
disease? Whatever your passion, there's a group out there
working to make your community a better place. Join them.
Call their office and ask to speak to a volunteer coordinator.
Most of the larger nonprofits have a range of committees—
from development (a fancy word for fund-raising) and marketing to special events and more—so there are a million ways
to get involved. In other words, don't be intimidated or think
you don't have a place. These organizations are always looking
for young professionals to carry their flag. And aside from the
obvious reward of contributing to the greater good, there's an
added professional benefit as well.

For example, let's say you work for a marketing firm and
you've just joined the communications team for the local
Red Cross. You're assigned to distribute press releases on an
upcoming education seminar. Now you're in a position to meet
the very media contacts you'll need to know in your day job.
It's truly a win-win situation.

Another advantage of volunteering is that it allows you to
meet and interact with other volunteers, some of whom will
be local luminaries. These are the business leaders in your
community—the presidents, managers, and chief something-
or-others—that you now have the privilege of working beside.
And there's nothing like community service to minimize the
hierarchy that's so prevalent in the workplace. For example,
if you're participating in a Habitat for Humanity building
project, it doesn't matter if the guy next to you is the president
of your state's largest bank; he's probably just as sweaty as you
are, and wondering how to put up the drywall too.

87 / Exit Gracefully

It happens to the best of us. You interviewed for the job you now hold, and it seemed like the perfect fit at the time. You bought into the company hype ("This place is going to be so much fun!") and you met lots of smiling faces on the tour ("I can totally work with these guys!"), so you signed on the bottom line and prepared yourself for greatness.

Now, it's almost a year later and your initial enthusiasm has dive-bombed faster than a kamikaze pilot. The work is torturously boring, your company champions fiefdoms over teamwork, and to top it off, your boss is a jerk who has yet to give you a job description, much less a projected career path. You're disillusioned and ready to make a change. Now what?

The first step is to realize that seemingly "wrong" jobs can be marvelous lessons in what *not* to do. You learn what kind of work makes you chew pencils all day, what kind of environment saps—rather than stimulates—your creativity, and perhaps even what kind of leader you don't want to be. All in all, this is incredibly valuable experience, so don't feel like you're wasting crucial career time.

Having said that, what *is* a waste of time is knowing that a job isn't right and continuing to stay on for months that turn into years. Before long, you start to accept that work is boring, turf wars are part of business, and you'll get promoted one of these days. If any of this sounds familiar, get out ASAP. Life is entirely too short to be miserable or achieve less than your highest potential. So how do you know when it's time to leave? Here are a few telltale signs:

- You don't have the freedom to do your best work.
- You've stopped learning.
- No one in management seems interested in you or your career.

- You no longer look forward to coming to work and you count down the minutes until five o'clock.

- Your office is a powder keg—that is, you never know who's going to blow next.

- Your company treats its staff like disposable minions, rather than valued contributors.

- You've answered the phone on numerous occasions when creditors or telemarketers are calling.

Regardless of why you've decided to bail, you owe it to yourself and your career to take the high road. This means bowing out of your current position with professionalism and class. The world is a very small place, and even if you think (or hope!) you will never see your boss or coworkers again, trust us, you probably will. Here are some etiquette guidelines for short timers:

- Give a minimum of two weeks' notice. Also, tell your boss before you inform any of your colleagues and ask how he would like to break the news.

- Create a detailed and easy-to-follow project notebook for every client (if you don't have one already).

- Write a status report on each of your assignments so your successor will know where you left off.

- Meet with colleagues to hand over your work and get the new team up to speed.

- Personally contact each of your customers to bid them farewell.

- Make sure all of your final tasks are complete, with no loose ends that will cause problems later.

- Engage in an exit interview with your management team and be honest, yet diplomatic in your responses.

- Resist any urges to bad-mouth the company and never post anything negative about your experience online.

If you follow these steps, you'll be able to walk out the door on your last day confident that you finished strong and left all things in good standing, including your reputation.

P.S. You'll know you're on the *right* career path when you're so passionate about your work that you'd do it for free if you could. Trust us, if you can get to this point in your career, the money will follow.

No Matter How Hot You Get, Never Burn a Bridge

For my first job, I worked for an international media juggernaut. My official title was "account management assistant," but a more accurate description would have been "underpaid, overworked personal gofer." When I wasn't running ridiculous errands for my boss, writing his reports for him, or covering for his frequent (and usually unexplained) absences, I was bitterly hunting for other jobs online. After a few months, I was offered a position at a smaller, local advertising agency and accepted in a heartbeat. I was ecstatic for two reasons: first, I was escaping my nine-to-five nightmare, and second, I could finally tell off my boss—something I had been looking forward to for a *very* long time.

Completely ignoring company protocol, I waited until my last day to notify my boss that I was leaving. I wrote a scathing letter, basically denouncing him for his unprofessional behavior and declaring that I was meant for bigger and better things. I left the letter on his desk and walked out the door, confident that I would never have to deal with him again. Wrong I was. A year after I left that job, my former company acquired the advertising agency. I was shuffled from department to department and ultimately ended up in my old division with my old boss as my new boss.

We eventually managed to patch things up— I apologized for my immature behavior and, much

continued

to my surprise, he apologized as well. We worked together for over a year, but there was always a lingering sense of awkwardness between us. That experience taught me an invaluable lesson: Always behave with professionalism and class, even if it means sacrificing short-term satisfaction. Since then, I've treated colleagues as if I'll be working with them for the rest of my career.

Sean O.
Business school student
Austin, Texas

88 / Final Self-Assessment

Remember: You'll never reach your career goals unless you know what they are. So find a nice quiet spot and take some time to record the following in your notebook:

- How long you've been at your job
- Your accomplishments
- What lessons you've learned
- The areas in which you've made the most improvement overall
- What you like best about your job so far
- What you like least about your job
- The most exciting, rewarding project you've worked on in the last year, and why
- What you would like your next position to be
- What skills you'll have to learn before you can be promoted to that role
- Your goals for the next six months
- Where you want to be in your career in two years and in five years

Congratulations! The very act of completing this self-assessment means that you are in the top five percent of *all* professionals. Now, get back to work.

EPILOGUE

If you have reached this point in the text, there's a good chance that you are well into your first real job. By now you've gained valuable insights about how to fit in, how to relate to others, and how to excel at work. You've earned the respect of your coworkers and clients, and demonstrated to your boss that you are hardworking, responsible, and reliable. If indeed you have put into practice everything we've shared with you—wow— you are one standout newbie. But what's next?

That first promotion beyond the entry level, the one to which you aspire, involves leadership. Conventional wisdom says that leaders are the ones who are the best at their jobs, right? That's part of it, but as we've pointed out, true leadership requires much more than talent. Effective leaders must be trustworthy. Inspirational. Dedicated. In fact, great leaders are like . . . a mirrored disco ball. Consider the following.

The Disco Ball Is Always Visible

True leaders don't hibernate in their office behind a closed door. They get out among the team, constantly coaching, conferring, and interacting.

The Disco Ball Never Stops Moving

Great leaders always press on, forge ahead, and remain undeterred by daily events, challenges, or adversity.

The Disco Ball Radiates Energy

Likewise, outstanding leaders enrich the environment for everyone, adding to the culture and vibrancy of their workplace.

The Disco Ball Never Changes

While the color, tempo, and frequency of the light beams change, the disco ball itself is solid and consistent. Similarly, admirable leaders are steadfast and dependable, no matter what the surrounding circumstances.

Finally, the Disco Ball Reflects Light

You will never hear a top-notch leader say, "Yes, it was a terrific success, and it was all my doing." The masterful leader, instead, understands the power of redirecting praise or credit to a deserving team. In the words of a great mentor, "Success isn't a me game, it's a we game."

See you at the top.

INDEX

ABOUT THE AUTHORS

Photo by K. D. Lett

A protégée and her mentor, Emily Bennington and Skip Lineberg help recent graduates bridge the gap between college and the workforce. Motivated by the premise that free coffee shouldn't be the sole highlight of a newbie's workday, Emily and Skip regularly host seminars on career success. Both authors live in Charleston, West Virginia.

During her first years in the workforce, EMILY BENNINGTON helped manage a successful Supreme Court Justice race and became the spokesperson for a business that was under intense public scrutiny. After navigating such sink-or-swim experiences with the guidance of her first boss, Skip Lineberg, Emily discovered that not all graduates are blessed with great mentors. Today she is a frequent speaker at universities and organizations on the topic of career success, particularly advancing the skills of young women in the workplace and volunteering as a means of leadership development. Emily also teaches a graduate course on social media and hosts a popular career blog at www.ProfessionalStudio365.com. She is a member of the CAREEREALISM team of career experts and contributes regularly to business publications and blogs on professional development issues.

As a career newbie, SKIP LINEBERG learned the art of successful management at General Electric during the Jack Welch heyday. Today he applies those skills as the owner of Maple Creative, a marketing firm staffed with more than a few young professionals. Under Skip's leadership, Maple has grown into a thriving business and garnered dozens of prestigious awards. Skip also hosts Maple's Marketing Genius blog, which *AdvertisingAge* magazine named one of the 150 most influential business blogs on the Web.

ABOUT COLLEGE SUMMIT

Hey, rock star! You've done more than buy a book. Since a portion of the proceeds for *Effective Immediately* benefit College Summit, you've helped your career *and* supported a great cause.

College Summit is a national organization that partners with public schools to increase college enrollment rates. Founded in 1993, College Summit has grown from working with four students in the basement of a low-income housing project to serving twenty-five thousand students annually at partner high schools in twelve states (California, Colorado, Connecticut, Florida, Indiana, Maryland, Missouri, New York, North Carolina, South Carolina, Virginia, and West Virginia) and Washington, D.C. The organization has been recognized as the U.S. Social Entrepreneur of the Year at the World Economic Forum in Davos, Switzerland, and has received five consecutive *Fast Company* Social Capitalist Awards.

College Summit's inside-the-school, serve-all-seniors approach is unique among college access providers. The organization helps students and schools leverage the assets they already have to create affordable, sustainable solutions. This model includes training influential students to ignite interest in college among their peers, equipping teachers to serve as change agents, developing a culture in which college is an expectation, and providing a postsecondary planning curriculum with hands-on, web-based technology. A recent independent analysis found that, when working with a full senior class, College Summit partner high schools saw a 20 percent increase in college enrollment compared to just a 4 percent increase for low-income students in general.

College Summit is driven by the belief that sending one student to college improves his or her life, sending a group of students to college strengthens communities, and making the college-enrollment process work for *all* students transforms generations. Ongoing support will allow College Summit to continue reaching out to the country's underserved high schools so that all of America's youth have the opportunity to achieve college and career success.

For more information, visit www.collegesummit.org.